Beyond Relativism

Beyond Relativism

Comparability in Cultural Anthropology

Robert C. Hunt

ALTAMIRA
PRESS

A DIVISION OF
ROWMAN & LITTLEFIELD PUBLISHERS, INC.
Lanham • New York • Toronto • Plymouth, UK

ALTAMIRA PRESS
A division of Rowman & Littlefield Publishers, Inc.
A wholly owned subsidary of The Rowman & Littlefield Publishing Group, Inc.
4501 Forbes Boulevard, Suite 200
Lanham, MD 20706
www.altamirapress.com

Estover Road
Plymouth PL6 7PY
United Kingdom

British Library Cataloguing in Publication Information Available

Library of Congress Cataloguing-in-Publication Data
Hunt, Robert C.
  Beyond relativism : comparability in cultural anthropology / Robert C. Hunt.
    p. cm.
  Includes bibliographical references and index.
  ISBN-13: 978-0-7591-1079-3 (cloth)
  ISBN-10: 0-7591-1079-4 (cloth)
  ISBN-13: 978-0-7591-1080-9 (pbk.)
  ISBN-10: 0-7591-1080-8 (pbk.)
  1. Cross-cultural studies. I. Title.

GN345.7.H86 2007
306—dc22   2006102315

This book is dedicated to my paternal grandfather, James Gallaway Hunt, who stimulated a life-long interest in serious books in a small boy.

Contents

~

Preface

You can't compare those; it's like comparing apples and oranges.

A frequently cited metaphor for inappropriate comparison in the United States evokes apples and oranges. Apples and oranges is about the impossibility of comparing two different things in a valid way.

But there is no inquiry, and no knowledge, without comparison. Comparison is asking questions of two or more instances. We ask whether the instances are the same or different. If they are the same we try to perceive in what ways they are the same. If they are different we try to perceive how they are different. And we almost always ask about the meaning of the sameness and the differences.

If we are a rabbit in an open field, we pay close attention to the sky. An empty sky, and a sky that has objects in it, are very different. A sky that is empty is safe for the moment. A sky that contains some floating or flying objects may not be safe. A sky that contains a falling leaf may be safe. A sky that contains a Golden Eagle is not safe. The differences are crucial, and have profound implications for the rabbit. They are the result of comparison.

All animal life makes constant comparisons of the environment. All animal life reacts to some conditions of the environment, and does not react to other conditions. Accurate observation of the environment is central to success. The wrong perception may well mean death of the self. Comparison is thus at the center of successful animal behavior.

All scholarly disciplines use comparison all the time. This is as true of literary studies as it is of art history, sociology, politics, psychology, biology, and physics. In common with the rest of the animal kingdom, success for humans means being able to make accurate comparisons, in our scholarly pursuits as well as in deciding when it is safe to cross the street.

Accurate comparison tells us something useful about the world. A precondition of accurate comparison is that our observations are comparable.

This book addresses the challenges to comparability in a scientific study of culture. Scientific anthropology searches for regularities in human behavior. Regularities are manifest in correlations. Correlations require valid and reliable observations of empirical phenomena. The methodological and epistemological conditions necessary for a science, then, require acceptable empirical observation. All of these observations are comparisons. And all valid observations demand comparability. Every challenge to comparability is therefore a challenge to our disciplines, and especially to those that are, or would be, sciences.

A scientific cultural anthropology has to be able to compare cultures. Relativist challengers to a science of culture hold that different cultures fit the metaphor of apples and oranges—they are incomparable. If that is true, it follows that no science of culture is logically possible. The issue is thereby joined.

Apples and oranges, according to the metaphor, are incomparable. They differ in the amount of vitamin C, taste of the skin, climate where the tree grows, pollination system, and in the meanings associated with them. To an American (of my generation) the apple is a central metaphor (apple of my eye, apple blossom time, Johnny Appleseed, motherhood and apple pie, apple pie order, etc.) while the orange has few associations. Apples and oranges are complex and different.

At the same time, the proposition that apples and oranges are incomparable is absurd. Of course one can compare apples and oranges—both are fruit, both grow on trees, both contain vitamins and minerals, prices can be expressed in terms of money per weight, or money per piece, and so forth. Apples and oranges are thus compared on a number of dimensions, and on these various dimensions they differ.

The solution to the problem of comparing apples and oranges is to first establish that "apples" and "oranges" are the same kind of object: they are both fruit. Second, we need to analyze apples and oranges with dimensions, such as kind of plant they grow on, seasonality, climate, color, amount of water, amount of vitamin C, amount of calories contained, and so on. Each of these dimensions has to be the same thing when it is applied to the objects, the apples and the oranges. Establishing both kinds of "sameness," of object and of dimension, is the key to comparability.

The problem of the comparison of apples and oranges is an apt metaphor for the problems of comparison not only for culture, but in all the sciences. When we effectively compare apples and oranges we solve all of these problems. How this is done is complex, interesting, and generalizable. The answers will take us into the heart of empirical observation in science, and from there to practice in scientific cultural anthropology. I will not only show that we do compare apples and oranges, I will show how it is done.

This book addresses the problem of achieving comparability in our observations of cultural phenomena. If success can be demonstrated, then a substantial challenge to, and problem for, a scientific cultural anthropology will be solved.

Part I lays out the principal challenges to comparability. Part II is concerned with natural science, and especially the structure of empirical observations, for both dimensions and objects. It demonstrates that the challenges laid out in part I are found in the natural sciences, and shows how the challenges have been met. Scientific Empirical Observation Languages (SEOLs) are the outcome, and they all utilize a small number of general principles.

Part III demonstrates that problems of comparable observation have been solved in some domains of culture, and that the solutions found there use the same principles as the ones used in the natural sciences. Chapter 5 concerns phonology; chapter 6, ethnobiology. Chapter 7 presents the current standards for agricultural productivity. Chapter 8 presents the beginnings of a Scientific Empirical Observation Language for the description of the social structure of canal irrigation, using the previously identified principles. Chapter 9 addresses kinship.

Part IV summarizes the argument for scientific empirical observation in cultural anthropology, demonstrates that there is good reason to entertain the idea of a social science, and refutes the claim that science is merely "western" ethnoscience.

Comparability is the key concept for our story. The message of the apples and oranges metaphor is that things are not comparable because they are different. As the story unfolds then we will see that while the metaphor of apples and oranges poses the problem, the problem has been solved over and over again in many domains, and with just a few basic principles.

Acknowledgments

This manuscript has been many years in the making. A number of people have read at least one version of it and given me good advice: Michael Porter, Melissa Hunt, Garth Isaak, Irene Winter, Donald Attwood, Davydd Greenwood, David Kaplan, Melford Spiro, Lawrence Kuznar, and anonymous reviewers. Pieces of the argument have been chewed over by several generations of students. My gratitude to them all, and they are in no way responsible for remaining errors and infelicities.

PART I

ARE CULTURES LIKE APPLES AND ORANGES?

The so-called science wars of the past couple of decades have been heated. Critiques of science have been vigorously presented, and vigorously responded to. Among the claims are that science is not objective, is not value-free, and has not produced unbiased knowledge of the world. This is because science is claimed to be only a social construction and therefore is presenting social interests rather than an objective account of reality. These claims assert that the results of science are not necessarily a reflection of nature's truth, and that the process is far from the "objective" one that many scientists claim it is.

Of course, if sciences cannot exist, then it is not possible for anthropology to have scientific procedures. But if one takes the position that physics, or biology, can be scientific, there is still the question of whether the subject matter of anthropology, the behavior of humans, is amenable to scientific procedures.

The science wars have long been present in anthropology as well. Elman Service, in his book A Century of Controversy (1985), argues that the dispute over the possibility of science in anthropology starts at least as early as the mid-nineteenth century. Recent attacks on the scientific possibility for anthropology have added the science wars concerns, and have been vigorous and widespread. And so now are the responses (see Spiro 1984, 1986; Reyna 1994; Kuznar 1997; Lett 1997; Cronk 1999; Harris 1999; Stephen J. Gould 2000; Bernard 2002; Sidky 2003).

This book addresses one of the issues in these wars, that of comparability of empirical observations. This is a fundamental issue, for if there is no comparability of empirical observations, there can be no science.

CHAPTER ONE

∼

A Scientific Cultural Anthropology?

Scientific *Cultural* Anthropology

Most of what we now call the "social sciences" (sociology, political science, economics, social psychology) are disciplines largely devoted to the study of *Homo sapiens* living in modern states (and usually Euro-American ones at that). There are other disciplines (linguistics, history, historical archaeology) which look at *Homo sapiens* living in many kinds of states, and one discipline (anthropology) that takes all hominids as its focus. (There are two other social sciences, ethology and ecology, whose subjects are social systems that sometimes include *Homo sapiens*, but these disciplines are, in America, normally found in schools of science, not schools of social science.)

Of all the social animals, humans produce the most variation in their behavior. If a social science of humans wants to make claims to generalize about *Homo sapiens* (or hominids), then the evidence must be systematically collected from the fullest possible range of human societies. Among the human sciences it is the anthropologists (including linguistic anthropologists, archaeological anthropologists, and sociocultural anthropologists) who have systematically collected and analyzed empirical evidence from the greatest variety of human societies.

We anthropologists study and produce knowledge of socially learned, traditional behavior. Contemporary *Homo sapiens* as a species is a social, symbolic, linguistic, and learning-driven animal. We are born into groups, live in groups, and die in groups. We are the most language-intensive species, the

3

species that uses and depends the most upon using symbols, and what we do is more dependent upon learning than any other species. The general term for this concept, at least in the English-speaking world, has been *culture*, a keyword for many anthropologists. Humans are born into and live in culture, and much of what we do is a product of, or is, culture, or cultural behavior.

How we think about and define culture makes a great deal of difference in how we think about a scientific cultural anthropology. There are many uses of the term *culture* at the end of the twentieth century. We have public culture, high culture, mass culture, and popular culture, as well as the cultures of agriculture, drugs, alcohol, and corporations. One wonders whether there is a common core of meaning in all these uses.

For much of the twentieth century *culture* was a technical term used largely by the discipline of anthropology. During the last third of the twentieth century the term became seriously ambiguous in the field. There are now two quite distinct sets of meanings for *culture* in anthropology. (The discussion of the two cultures that follows owes much to Lett 1987.)

Some hold that culture refers to all socially learned behavior and is principally but not exclusively a human attribute (culture1). Others hold that culture is the system or web of meanings that humans generate (culture2). This latter view is widely represented among conceptual relativists. The differences between these two uses have implications for the possibility of a science of culture.

Culture1 derives from E. B. Tylor's book on culture, published in 1871. The opening lines of his book are:

> Culture or Civilization, taken in its wide ethnographic sense, is that complex whole which includes knowledge, belief, art, morals, law, custom, and any other capabilities and habits acquired by man as a member of society. The Condition of culture among the various societies of mankind, in so far as it is capable of being investigated on general principles, is a subject apt for the study of laws of human thought and action. (Tylor 1871:1)

This concept of culture includes everything that a human does that is learned as a member of a society. Myths, rituals, songs, ideas about life after death, as well as the particular languages, crops grown, and appropriate spatial distances that strangers maintain with respect to one another, are all equally parts of culture. There are few regularities in human social behavior that are not included in culture1.[1]

The second concept of culture, culture2, is a much smaller set of human experience. In Keesing's analysis this is partitioned into cognitive, structure of mental concepts, and symbolism (Lett 1987:56). There are substantial differences between these three approaches. What they have in common is that culture is assigned primarily, if not exclusively, to the interior of the organism, rather than in the behavior of the organism. They are all varieties of an idealist approach to the matter, which refers to the concepts or categories held and articulated by the members of a society. It is often called the meaning system of the members of that society. This approach to culture is an old one in American anthropology. It is clearly seen in a famous article of Sapir's published in 1929, and Redfield in 1934 referred to culture as the "shared understandings" held by members of a community (Sapir 1929; Redfield 1934).

Culture2 became much more prominent in American anthropology with the publications of Clifford Geertz starting in 1973 (Geertz 1973). Two of the most visible advocates of this view of culture are Geertz and David Schneider, both of them students at Harvard when Talcott Parsons was a major intellectual force in the social sciences in the United States. The Parsonian framework partitioned human experience so that "action" is the prime phenomenon to be examined. "Action" is restricted to intentional behavior and may be analytically partitioned into social, cultural, personality, and organism dimensions.

In the Parsonian framework, culture is the meaning system and is therefore closely akin to culture2 (see Kroeber and Parsons 1958). Melford Spiro presents the most articulate view of the Parsonian paradigm in contemporary anthropology (Spiro 1984, 1986). Spiro is clear that culture refers to culture2 but that other dimensions which affect human behavior must be kept in mind. He refers to society, personality (a major interest of his), ecology, and the economy. Culture, then, for Spiro is only a part of what culture1 is for others.

There is a variant of culture2 presented by Ward Goodenough (1996 and many other places), who refers to culture as "the *knowledge* people must have in order to function acceptably as members of an interacting group in the contexts in which they interact" (1996, emphasis added). Goodenough refers to this as the ideational order.

It seems useful to separate the internal states of the organisms from the behavior of the organism. There is no doubt that all behavior, and all social behavior, requires motivated and competent organisms. It would be quite wonderful to have a detailed and accurate understanding of motivated states of organisms. But it would seem that propositions about those states (including language instinct, rational action, selfish gene, Malinowski's needs, and Goodenough's knowledge) require many assumptions and long, fragile chains of inferences. These motivated states are very hard to investigate directly. I claim that at this point in time the public behavior is far more accessible and yields far more readily to empirical observation.

Humans learn culture in small face-to-face groups, and we start no later than birth to do that learning. That local system of what we learn can be called a natural culture. Each natural culture has a set of concepts, ideas, and meanings (part of culture2). How these natural culture concepts relate to science is a tangled and complex issue that has deeply divided scholars of the human condition. It is a central issue for the question of constructing a scientific cultural anthropology.

Everybody agrees that natural culture (often called folk culture) categories exist. Some contend that there is only one kind of system, folk systems, and that what passes for Western science is really just a Western folk system. There are others who contend that there is a significant difference between folk systems, including Western folk systems,[2] and science.

If there are only folk concepts, and if culture is restricted to culture2, there is no reason to expect there to be analytic segments of the world which are shared by more than a few folk cultures. If this is so, comparable observation of empirical reality becomes unlikely, and so valid systematic comparison is unlikely, and therefore arriving at nomothetic propositions becomes unlikely. Therefore, a science of culture is improbable.

If, however, we can construct a set of concepts that are not folk categories but which transcend folk categories, then science becomes not just another folk system but something radically different. The challenge for a science of culture, then, is to construct a set of concepts for observation of the empirical realm of culture in such a way that we can justify calling it a science of culture.

The nature of a science of culture also depends on whether culture1 or culture2 is being used. It is possible to conceive of a science of culture2, and Hanson (1975) and Spiro (1984, 1986) have argued for its existence. But such a science would be one of ideas, meanings, and the like. In the event that one wants to construct a science of culture2, one should also consider what one does about concepts such as society, personality, and ecology. They would not automatically be included in a study of culture2.

It is also possible to conceive of a science of culture1. In this case, the meaning system would be a part of culture, along with economic structure, politics, religion, disease and medical patterns, and so forth. The domain of culture1 is much larger than the domain of culture2.

Many anthropologists are committed to using culture to name culture2. Adam Kuper's Culture (1999) and the special issue of Current Anthropology entitled Culture—A Second Chance? (also 1999) refer only to culture2. Sperber's book Explaining Culture takes the same position (1996). Often called interpretivists, most scholars committed to the culture2 version show a good deal of resistance to claims about a science of culture (see Rabinow and Sullivan 1987; Rosaldo 1989; Tyler 1987). Some of the challenges to comparability derive from this position.

At the same time, a substantial number of anthropologists are committed to using culture to name culture1. (See Marvin Harris's *Theories of Culture in Postmodern Times* [1999], especially chapter 1.) It is this set that makes most of the claims for a scientific cultural anthropology. Some of the challenges to comparability come from this persuasion.

In the endeavor that is called scientific cultural anthropology there are two general kinds of project: describing local realities and comparing local realities.

Local Reality

A major characteristic of empirical investigations in anthropology is that a great deal of effort is invested in investigation of a local reality. The excavation in archaeology, the field investigation of language, the fieldwork of social and cultural anthropologists and of animal behaviorists, all invest a large number of hours of work in a relatively small place. The focus is local and highly detailed.

The scientific anthropologist's first project is to get that local reality right. By *anthropologist* here I refer to the cultural and linguistic anthropologist doing fieldwork, and the archaeologist excavating a site. The total collection of investigations of local reality produce a picture of detail and, overall, variation. No two local realities are identical (however similar they might be). In sociocultural anthropology this project has been called ethnography (after Lowie) by Murdock and many others. There are problems of comparability involved, for the initial observations, and the subsequent reports, ought to achieve comparability.

Comparing Local Realities

Scientific cultural anthropology also has comparative projects, in which we attempt to generalize over two or more of the local reality studies. These comparative projects demand comparability of the results of the field projects.

Multilocal Systems

One type of comparative project is to establish multilocal systems, such as Nuer, Anasazi, or a language such as Nahuatl. These areal systems are larger in territorial scope than a single local reality. The syntheses that emerge are often more complex than any single local reality. We look for indicators of economic, political, or religious systems that tie these various local points to-gether. We look for a state, or a society, or a culture, in which all these local reality points participate(d). Larger and more complex social systems show more local specialization. (Few practitioners have discussed the serious methodological or epistemological challenges in this effort [but see Adams and Adams 1991].) The major constraint has been to find enough local data points to justify the effort of synthesis.

Correlations of Dimensions

Another kind of comparative project is to search for correlations in the re-lationships of dimensions among a sample, or all, of these local or regional sys-tems. For instance, the relationship between kinship and politics, between food production technology and social complexity, between child-rearing practices and the concepts of the supernatural, have been investigated, and there are hundreds of other possibilities (Tylor 1889; see Narroll 1970b, Levinson and Malone 1980, and Ember and Levinson 1991 for surveys of the results). These comparisons search for regularities in the variation but are not focused on a single local unit. Instead the focus in this type of project is on the correlation of a small number of dimensions over a large number of local units.

Evolution

Another comparative project in the social sciences is the study of secular development of variation in capacities and behavior of humans. Often called evolution, there is an interest in the origins and development of domestica-tion of plants and animals, of cities, of states, of the diffusion of these phe-nomena to other groups, and of what difference this makes for other phe-nomena (see Johnson and Earle 1987 for an example). The popularity of this form of study varies from decade to decade within anthropology, yet it never seems to disappear as a question which excites the efforts of some of us.

Human Nature

Another kind of comparative project is to search for phenomena univer-sal to the species (or higher levels of taxonomy) (see Brown 1991 for an ac-count). Often called human nature, this project is the hardest to accomplish. A variant attempts to place *Homo sapiens* in nature, with serious continuities as well as discontinuities across species borders. Earl Count (1973) was an early exemplar. Some ethologists, sociobiologists, evolutionary psychologists, and linguists have been interested in this project. The demands on research design are enormous. The comparability challenges across species boundaries of this project are especially difficult to solve.

Ethology

The comparative study of the behavior of living nonhuman animals is another generalizing project in the social sciences in which some anthropologists participate. Some of this behavior is almost certainly not learned and socially transmitted, but some of it apparently is. In a recent review McGrew found unequivocally that learned and socially transmitted behavior is found among several species of nonhuman primates (particularly chimpanzees— *Pan troglodytes*) (McGrew 1998:301–328). Whiten et al. (1999) conducted a comparative study of chimpanzee (*Pan troglodyte*) behavior and found evidence for cultural variation among six study sites in Africa.

There is a vigorous argument over whether animals other than humans have culture. By culture the "animal behavior" students are clearly using culture1. It is hard to even imagine how such a debate could take place if culture2 was the key term. Much depends upon whether the distribution of "culture" is assigned by fiat in a definition (usually limited to a set of language-using humans), or whether the definition is independent of the distribution which then becomes an empirical issue.

Other kinds of comparative efforts have been actively pursued from time to time. Early in the twentieth century the possible correlations of culture with language, race, and environment were investigated, and the negative result has been widely accepted (perhaps too casually). In the second half of the twentieth century the Weber-Parsons model of social science has had a great deal of influence. It partitioned human action into several systems, including culture2, society, economy, and personality. Each of these systems was investigated for its own properties, and on occasion variation in each of the dimensions was to be studied for correlations with variation in the other dimensions. What remains today is an impression of concentrated effort within systems. In the last quarter of the twentieth century there was a strong effort to articulate biology, psychology, and the study of human behavior. Evolutionary psychology, one part of that effort, has been primarily interested in phenomena asserted to be produced by natural selection, hardwired in the human brain and thus to be part of human nature.

The human nature project of cultural anthropology provides us with many opportunities to exercise our skills at research design. We should amass widespread evidence, across many different cultures, of the existence of this phenomenon. What is needed for each and every claim of content of human nature is a thorough combing of the comparative ethnographic literature, and close reasoning about the relationship between this posited piece of human nature and culture1. With respect to the capacity for natural language we have plentiful evidence that virtually all humans have it, for every society has at least one natural language, many have two or more, and virtually all members of the society (who live to adulthood) learn to become competent speakers of at least one natural language. This to me is strong evidence that a language instinct exists for *Homo sapiens*.

When we come to a template for ANIMAL, however, there is the possibility that this is a product of culture1, and not of human nature. It seems clear that there is a template for NUMBER (it is found in infants, monkeys, and other species [Gelman and Gallistel 2004]). However, there is a need to be precise. The number template is for an approximate quantity. Precise quantities, even for the number one, are not universally found among humans (see Gordon 2004; Gelman and Gallistel 2004; Pica et al. 2004). NUMBER thus has two meanings, and the meanings must be specified if the claims about human nature are to be accepted.

The ontological issue that these various efforts present is how we are to conceptualize the structure of our study of human behavior. Taxonomies are useful as an aid in thinking this through. If we say that culture1 is all socially learned behavior, then how is culture1 placed in a taxonomy? It must be at some level, and there must be other taxa at the same level. Presumably that level would also contain instinct, idiosyncratic behavior, nonsocially learned behavior, and perhaps others. For some of these taxa we know a great deal about the internal organization. But I know of no effort to be exhaustive at this level of the taxonomy. The next higher level needs to be named and defined and its members identified. There is much work to be done.

Three of our generalizing projects—the correlational one, the evolutionary one, and the human nature one—are the primary location of the nomothetic effort in scientific cultural anthropology. It follows that culture1 is the more effective approach. If the culture2 approach is utilized, it would appear that there is nothing to say about developmental issues where there is no writing. They are precluded by definition, as there will be little or no evidence about meaning systems to process. This applies as well to the comparative study of culture across species, where the absence of language makes it very difficult to get more than tiny fragments of the mental life of nonhuman species in a natural setting.

Scientific Cultural Anthropology

This book starts from the premise that knowledge for its own sake is feasible, legitimate, and possible. There is a long history of this position, and although the assumption has been rejected by some, it is accepted by many others. I assume that scientific knowledge is desirable quite independent of the uses to which it might be put (see Gross and Plattner 2002).

The term *knowledge* has been used in many different contexts. There are references to folk knowledge, intuitive knowledge, different ways of knowing (by gender, by ethnicity), to insider and outsider knowledge. The terrain is balkanized.

This book addresses one form of knowledge, the one modified by *scientific*. As contested as science and the scientific are in some quarters, I start from the position that science is (so far) the most effective way to acquire knowledge of many kinds of reality external to the self. The sciences have a long and justly celebrated history of accomplishment.

One of the more hotly contested ideas has been that of science applied to human social behavior. A variety of reasons have been brought forward in arguing against that possibility, and the question of comparability of human behavioral phenomena ranks very high on this list. The reasonable social scientist must consider whether there are plausible challenges to the enterprise, and if plausible challenges are found they must be dealt with.

There are many features of scientific knowledge. Since we are concentrating on comparability, only some of those features need to be in focus.

Scientific knowledge of human social behavior can be described as statements about a social reality external to the investigator that have intersubjective reliability and validity, have logical consistency, are correlations with reasonably low levels of uncertainty attached to them, generalize, and at their best explain aspects of that reality. These statements are produced with an epistemology that is skeptical, has canonical standards of replication, and is committed to identifying and excising errors.

Science is nomothetic. It attempts to discover regularities in the form of correlations, and then relationships of cause and effect.[3] In each particular science the goal is to find general principles which account for (explain, determine) much of the phenomena within some domain. There is considerable range of the domain over which a generalization applies. Some disciplines (e.g., nuclear physics) attempt to generalize over the whole universe for all known time periods. But narrower domains are also legitimate. Primate evolution is presently limited to the most recent geological eras, and to this planet. Historically there have been efforts to expand the size of the domain, and to find principles which are universally applicable in the domain.

Science is empirical in the sense that it is about some reality external to the observer, the generalizations and explanations are about that reality, and the generalizations are tested on evidence from that reality. I do not assert that there is a single true reality. I do take the position that there are events that take place outside of, in the absence of, and without the participation of, any observer. Science is the effort to observe, measure, describe, analyze, and ultimately try to explain any order found in those events. Science, in this view, is "about" that reality. And that external reality thereby constrains the results.

Every science of course will contain some propositions that are about research design, or definitions and assumptions, and that are not about that external empirical reality. But the substantive focus of the science is reality, the objective is to describe and find explanations for some of that reality, and the empirical evidence is necessary. A science must be able to observe that empirical reality. Observations[4] of it must be systematic, and must be both reliable and valid. Reliability refers to the ability to repeat a measuring procedure and get the same result. Validity refers to whether the measure is actually observing what it is claimed to be observing. Both are evaluated by correlations. Reliability is evaluated by the correlation of two measures of the same thing. Validity is evaluated by the correlation between a measure and a different criterion (sometimes a much more expensive and precise measure of the same phenomenon). Note that both of these procedures require systematic comparison. Larger numbers of accurate and precise observations are better than smaller numbers, but accuracy and precision are more important than sheer volume.

The systematic comparisons necessary for correlations are dependent upon successful observation of the empirical realm. Scientific Empirical Observation Languages (SEOLs) systematically structure and record observations of the empirical realm. They are required in every science, and scientists must strive to achieve comparability.

Scientific observation of reality is analytical in the sense that the flow of experience is divided into segments. These segments are named, and the segments are assumed to occur in more than one instance. Some of these segments are objects, like planets, apples and oranges, and chemical elements, and sometimes these objects are placed in taxonomies (e.g., biological systematics, periodic table).

Some of the segments are dimensions of things, such as length, mass, atomic weight, and color, which are usually presented as variables.[5] Scientists construct categories of objects that identify kinds of objects, and they construct variables which observe dimensions of those objects. In science there is a strong effort to have the particular concepts of objects and dimensions constrained by reality. Scientists also strive to find words to unambiguously label the concepts (of objects, dimensions, and values on dimensions). That is, we try to achieve a one-to-one relationship between a word, a concept, and a partition of reality. All scientists assume that in principle both kinds of segmentation (objects, dimensions) should be valid, and constrained by external reality. The objects, the dimensions, and their names must be comparable across instances.

Science is thus necessarily comparative. The regularities sought (and found) can only be found by means of comparison. One meaning of comparison in the science context is that each of a specified number of objects (say, galaxies, elephants, or societies) is observed for each of a specified number of dimensions (such as distance, mass, kinship terminology). The correlations we seek cannot be accepted or rejected unless this systematic comparison is performed. No claim of a pattern or relationship of variables will be accepted in science without the evidence being part of a well-constructed systematic comparison.

There is another key meaning of comparison. Every recorded observation is a comparison, in that the classifying of the perception is dependent upon a comparison of the external object with some sort of standard. The perception is thus compared with the appropriate standard (see Kaplan and Manners 1972).

The generalizing projects of a scientific anthropology, involving as they do dozens or hundreds of studies of local realities, must face comparability problems squarely. Vigorous, and sometimes significant, challenges to our ability to compare across the local realities have been offered. If the challenges to comparison are not solved, the results of the generalizing efforts are uncertain and of probably dubious value. If the challenges to comparison are not met satisfactorily, there can be no social science.

Apples and oranges are compared by establishing kinds of objects, and kinds of dimensions. It is hard to imagine how correlations can be produced without having several dimensions in the first place. If this reasoning is sound, then a scientific study of human cultural behavior also requires objects and dimensions (and of course they have to be comparable). At this point in the argument I assert that the objects for a scientific anthropology are the local systems of social behavior, variously called societies, cultures, or communities. The dimensions are the phenomena we call language, kinship, economy, political relationships, religion, and so forth. I will have more to say about this in part III and will come back to it in part IV. My hope is that the reader will at this stage agree for the sake of the argument, and wait to see how it works out.

Notes

1. It has been clear for a century or more that much of the variability in human behavior is not caused by "race," natural language, or environment. It has instead sometimes been said to be caused by culture. But culture has been used as an overall description of the regularities and variations that we have observed. Can culture cause itself? There is work yet to be done on this question.

2. The existence of a single "Western culture" has been casually assumed, and used, by a great many. James Carrier has been arguing that it is not clear that there is a single Western folk model (1992, 1995).

3. At this point in human history causal statements about human social behavior are not characterized by low levels of uncertainty. We are still at the stages of description and correlation (but see for example Vayda 1989). But as will be shown below, we do in fact have reasonably reliable and valid methods of description in some realms, and some reasonably robust correlations. There is good reason to be optimistic about the idea of a social science that discovers cause and effect relationships.

4. Measurement is a special case of observation, one that applies when dimensions have been constructed as mature variables. All knowledge is based on comparison, and therefore comparability is always a factor. Measurement is a special case of comparison. All measurement requires comparison, and therefore comparability. Comparison (and observation) can occur without measurement, but not the reverse.

5. Variables are special cases of dimensions. See discussion in chapter 3.

CHAPTER TWO

~

Challenges to Comparability

The metaphor of apples and oranges claims that comparability is a feature of sameness, and since apples and oranges are different, they are not comparable. However, it has been shown that apples and oranges *can* be compared.

Comparability is achieved by constructing concepts of the same *kind* of thing, not identical things. Apples and oranges are both fruit, and therefore the same *kind* of thing, and therefore comparable. The same argument applies to the dimensions. If we are to compare the amount of vitamin C in apples and oranges, vitamin C has to have the same definition in each application for it to be the same (kind of) dimension. Furthermore, we need a unique name for each concept. Otherwise it is very difficult to be sure which concept is being referred to.

Comparability is achieved when we have valid concepts for the same kinds of objects, valid concepts for the same kinds of dimensions, and unique names for each of the concepts.

Achieving that sameness of kind for culture is not easy. Indeed, some argue that it is impossible. Leach asserted that kinds of cultural things do not exist:

> Cultural facts are not readily discriminated into ultimate units which can be given precise taxonomic description. . . . Social reality could . . . be described as a system of relationships between unit traits which recur in different cultural contexts, just as unit atoms of particular elements recur in different chemical contexts. This orientation to cultural data is untenable. The units of ordinary

anthropological description—expressions like "patrilineal descent," "uxorilo-
cal residence," "matrilateral cross-cousin marriage," "ancestor worship," "bride-
price," "shifting cultivation," etc. . . . are not in any way comparable to the precisely defined diagnostic elements which form the units of discourse in natural
science. This is the heart of the whole matter. (Leach 1965:340–341)

Leach's assertion could have been based on one or more of a number of arguments concerning the lack of comparability.

Natural Culture Uniqueness

It is sometimes said that every culture is unique and therefore it follows that
no scientific procedures can be imagined (see Scholte 1984:963). As with apples and oranges, uniqueness implies incomparability.

Uniqueness seems to mean a lack of identity. One meaning of identity is
that one entity can be exactly mapped onto another. If there is *any* difference
between them, two cultures are not identical. Note that if two entities share
99 percent of their content, by this definition they are still unique, for 1 percent is *not* shared. They are unique, then, only in the sense of not being exactly and entirely the same. They cannot be compared, in the sense of comparison that demands identity. And if they cannot be compared, they are not
fit subjects for a (transcultural) social science.

The difficulty this poses for a science would be overwhelming. But the difficulty is a function of the meaning of identity. Science does rely on identities, but of a different type. All of the sciences (and all of our disciplines) rely
on the identification of *kinds* of entities (e.g., novels, rice plants, mammals).
The kind of thing has to be an identity in every comparison. All things called
elephant must share "elephantness," and nothing that has or manifests "elephantness" can be left out of the category. Of course no two elephants are totally identical to each other, and the same is true of moons, tides, and spears.
In science we must be able to establish the identities of kinds, and then we
turn to observing, measuring, and explaining some similarities and differences among the examples.

These classes of objects are achieved by finding some explicit criterion
which is common to them all. The identity is in the definition and operation
of that criterion, not in the objects as wholes. Clearly, then, the search for total identity of natural objects or events is usually fruitless. Identity is necessary
for the kind of object, and for the dimensions (and the values on the dimensions) of those natural objects. A measure of pH must be identical *in definition*
every time it is applied, although the value on the dimension can of course

vary. Every meter stick is supposed to be identical to every other one. It is likewise with such things as temperature, liter, and form of residence.

Uniqueness of phenomena is not a problem. All of science works with two levels of comparison, with identical kinds of things (at one level), which then can vary (at a different level). Identity at the level of kind of thing is essential; identity at the level of the particular example is not. Indeed, if everything were identical at all levels there would be no science, and no need for science. Equally, if everything were unique at all levels there could be no science. Uniqueness of natural cultures is not a plausible challenge to the existence of kinds of cultural things.

Context and Natural Culture

A frequently heard objection to a scientific cultural anthropology is that the cross-cultural systematic comparisons tear the cultural facts from their context, thus destroying or distorting the meaning of those facts. Natural cultures are usually assumed to have systemic properties. Kinship, the family, and medical diagnosis and treatment are also treated as having systemic properties. There is little about natural culture that is not treated, at least part of the time, as being part of a system. It follows that what we know about any part of any natural culture "system" is in part a product of how that part relates to the other parts in the system.

The systematic comparisons that are the necessary procedure of any scientific endeavor operate analytically in the sense that they must isolate some elements. The comparison demands that the elements be taken from the wholeness of the context they are embedded in. When we isolate any part of any of these contexts, and do it for a large sample of such cultures (> 20), it is impossible to remember, much less put into the comparison, the complex relationships that the elements have to the other elements in the matrix where they originated.

The conclusions often drawn from these realizations are that (1) the systematic comparison destroys these contextual meanings, which is true; and (2) the systematic comparison is thereby rendered invalid, which I contend is not necessarily true.

It has to be granted that the contextual richness of a local cultural reality is lost in systematic comparisons. And that richness of connections, derived from concentrating on the local reality, is one of the triumphs of the anthropological enterprise. We continually show to a resistant world that other cultures, no matter what the technology or size of population, are rich and complex ways of life, as complex and rich in their way as our own. That

complexity must not be sacrificed: it is too important a contribution to act-
ing informedly and morally in a multicultural world. It is an important result
of the local reality project.

But it is conceivable that anthropologists could legitimately do two jobs.
We could, in our ethnographic project, emphasize local systems and local
complexity. And we could, in our comparative projects, take the elements of
these systems out of their individual contexts, and see if there are correlations between such elements. Any meaning we find in such systems of correlations is largely a product of the correlations we find and of the theory we
apply to them.

The meanings we extract from systematic comparisons are often surprising, and on occasion cascade into substantial complexities. For example, several comparativists have found that women are rarely responsible for guiding
a plow (Ember 1983). Carol Ember noted these facts, looked hard within her
set of variables for an explanation, and did not find one, which she noted
(Ember 1983). It is a correlation, but one without an explanation.

Morgan Maclachlan, in an ethnographic study of peasant agriculture in
India, looked into the matter, and his claim is that upper-body strength is
positively correlated with the quality of the plowing, and that the quality of
the plowing contributes positively to crop yield (Maclachlan 1983; Hunt
1988a). Finally, he finds that upper-body strength correlates with gender,
males having more of it. If Maclachlan is correct (and his work needs to be
replicated), we have the beginnings of an explanation for the very widespread phenomenon of men handling an animal-drawn plow and women not
handling these plows.

I suggest that the "meaning" of correlations increases when other correlations are linked to them. The more interlinked correlations we find, the
more "meaning" we have created. When we have a dense net of correlations
we have constructed a complex system, which is more meaningful than an
isolated correlation.

One such satisfying set of correlations contains the variables of population, population density, technology of production, agricultural surplus, kinds
of economic exchanges, division of labor, and complexity of political organization (see Johnson and Earle 1987 for a recent summary). Hunting and
gathering as the primary activity of production is almost everywhere associated with low population, low population density, high rates of spatial mo-
bility, no permanent settlements, low degree of division of labor, little or no
surplus, reciprocity in exchanges, an egalitarian society, and no formal political organization. Where intensive agriculture exists, it is very strongly associated with high population, high population densities, high degree of divi-

sion of labor, considerable agricultural surplus, exchanges dominated by redistribution and/or the market principle, stratification in society, and formal political organization.

We can see systems in societies that depend upon hunting and gathering, and systems in societies with intensive agriculture. The individual elements are of course torn from the original context, and thereby lose some meaning. But when the search for correlations is successful we rebuild systems of meaning, only in this case they are not connected to a single natural culture but to systems present in many local realities.

There is no doubt that we do not as yet know how to systematically compare large complex wholes. Our only mode of comparison, so far, is the analytic process of breaking the whole up into segments, and comparing segments. We can construct wholes by listing the segments, but we are still dealing with the segments. And there is no doubt that some meaning is lost when we take a segment from its original systemic context. All of this is true.

What, if any, are the consequences for comparability, and in consequence for a scientific anthropology? My answer is that there are none. The value of systematic comparison is shown in the results. If we can successfully construct systems of correlations by means of cross-cultural comparison, then what we have is at least as real as any imputed (or constructed) society or culture.[1] And, as Naroll (1970b), Levinson and Malone (1980), and Ember and Levinson (1991) have shown, we have found many such systems of correlations. Tambiah implies that preference for either the denseness of an ethnographic description or the wide range of a systematic comparison may be no more than a matter of taste (1990). If it is a matter of taste alone, then there is no rational imperative not to conduct systematic cross-cultural comparison. I contend that there is at least one good reason for supporting the search for sets of cross-cultural comparisons, and that reason is the past success in finding correlations. I reject the contextual argument against comparability for a scientific cultural anthropology.

Cultural Contamination of Concepts

Cultural contamination, or ethnocentrism, is a major problem for comparability. I suggest that there are strong and weak versions. The strong version, which is rooted in natural language determinism, holds that concepts and language are the same, and that there are only natural languages. The weak version is focused on ethnocentrism in our construction of scientific concepts.

Strong Version

Every natural culture contains many different concepts.[2] Some of them are analytic, in the sense that they segment the flow of experience into pieces (animals, trees, birds, humans, houses, gardens, dreams, etc.). Some of these concepts are quite technical and precise (the technical concepts used by navigators, gardeners, astronomers, etc.). The largest set of these from folk cultures that we know about in detail is probably the ethnobiological work by such researchers as Conklin, Berlin, Hunn, Bulmer, and Ellen. We have much yet to discover about these languages: how much ambiguity do they contain? What is their synchronic distribution (age, gender, specialties), and how stable are they in time? How is training to use them accomplished? (See the discussion in chapter 6.) There is no doubt that these concepts are not identical for all cultures. They are often called folk concepts.

Many have seen a very powerful connection, and perhaps an identity, between these folk concepts and the natural language of the society (Kuznar calls it linguistic determinism [1997:121–122]).

> The fact of the matter is that the "real world" is to a large extent unconsciously built up on the language habits of the group. . . . The worlds in which different societies live are distinct worlds, not merely the same world with different labels attached. (Sapir 1929:162)

This idea is also held by some philosophers. A general version of it was presented by Winch in his *Idea of a Social Science* in 1958:

> Our idea of what belongs to the realm of reality is given for us in the language we use. The concepts we have settle for us the form of the experience we have of the world. . . . there is no way of getting outside the concepts in terms of which we think of the world. . . . The world *is* for us what is presented in those concepts. (Winch 1958:15, emphasis in original)

Winch here is equating concepts and language, a position that many adopt. The language referred to is natural language. It follows that our ability to observe the empirical realm is constrained by the properties of natural language.[3]

Since natural languages differ, and natural cultures differ, folk "concepts" must also differ from culture to culture. The radical relativist position is that things themselves, as well as their meanings, differ from culture to culture.[4] The reasoning is that every human experience is structured by the culture of that human. And since every culture contains at least one symbolic system, and if symbol systems are assumed to be constructed sui generis by every culture, it follows that there is the possibility of no identity of meaning from one culture to another. It further follows that there is the possibility of no identity of experience as well (see Geertz 1983:160).[5]

If what we are concerned with is the meanings of things in natural cultures, and if these meanings are arbitrarily constructed, and if they differ from one culture to another, then that is the only generalization that any social science can hope to produce. If the "same things" are very unlikely to exist across cultural boundaries, there will be no comparability of these things across cultural boundaries, and in consequence no social science based on these meanings can exist. These differences in meaning are one reason to conclude that the same kinds of cultural things do not exist, and therefore there is a fundamental incomparability about human experiences in different places and times.

If it is true, as some assert, that the only concepts for apprehending the empirical domain are folk concepts, then there can be little chance for creating a scientific cultural anthropology. This is a version of the position that "science" is only Western ethnoscience. It will be argued below that science is indeed socially constructed, but it is not a construction of or by or in natural culture. There are substantial and significant differences between scientific and natural culture.

Everybody agrees that folk concepts exist. The question is whether it is possible to construct concepts/categories that are not folk categories.

If we can construct a set of concepts that transcend folk concepts but are not folk concepts, then science becomes not just another folk system but something different. A necessary condition for a science of culture is to construct a set of scientific concepts for observation and measurement of the empirical realm of culture. Ways to reduce the constraints of natural language and natural culture are needed.

We have been creating categories for apprehending the empirical domain (of culture) that are not folk concepts since at least 1871 (Morgan 1871; Tylor 1871). Curiously, while much effort has been invested, there has been relatively little discussion of the concept-construction process itself. An important feature of this process is the division of labor between informant and scientist in how the analysis of the local reality is done.

The difference between natural culture and scientific culture is important, so it will be useful to summarize how one comes to learn a scientific culture. Every human grows from infancy within at least one natural culture (some persons find themselves in a handful). Learning (of content and structure) begins in infancy and continues until death. Much of the natural culture is associated with one (or at most of a handful of) natural language(s) that was (were) learned starting in infancy. These natural cultures are constituted of structured traditional behavior, which by definition is learned socially. In contemporary natural cultures (of *Homo sapiens*) there is also a good deal of talk about some of that natural culture, and some of the natural culture consists of talk.

Every scientist is first enculturated in a natural culture. At a later point formal training in science begins. In the case of anthropology, as part of our formal training (usually beginning at the university stage of our education) we read, discuss, and write about the features of some local systems which are different from ours and different from each other. Associated with this effort is conscious consideration of the features of the natural culture in which that university is embedded. Also as part of our university training we are supposed to learn the content and methods then current in the discipline. As part of our disciplinary training we should also be exposed to the history of the discipline, learning that (and ideally how) the scientific framework has developed greater precision and validity over the decades. We also learn that in the course of this development cultural contamination has been reduced.

The next step (in professional education) is direct personal investigation of some local reality through fieldwork. In that experience we may learn more about our own natural culture as well, and perhaps discover that the scientific roster of concepts needs correction. Upon return to the university we think about, and write about, that local reality, making our results available in the public record. One of the goals is an account of the local reality studied. Another goal is to improve the set of scientific concepts, and the reader will find many examples in part III of this book.

The conjunction of the local reality and the scientifically trained observer involves talk about the locality in the local natural language(s), observable local behavior, awareness of the natural culture of the outside observer, and the scientific culture of the observer. There is always local talk about what is happening locally. There seems to be wide agreement that the local systems of talk partially map the local systems of behavior. Some of this talk makes quite good maps. But some of the talk makes errors of commission, and some of it makes errors of omission, often substantial errors.

We as scientific anthropologists (and other kinds of social scientists) have evolved sets of scientific concepts which describe in detail much of the talk and behavior in local realities. It has been under construction since at least 1871 in anthropology, it has developed, and we have identified and removed many items of cultural contamination.

The natural history of scientific concepts shows us that the vast majority of them originated in some natural culture. As they develop and are applied in new contexts, it becomes clear that there is contamination from one or more natural cultures. Such challenges can be responded to with modification of the concept to accommodate the new distinctions. Under this pressure the concept is continually refined until there is very little evidence of cultural contamination.

Scientific concepts are held and manipulated by only a few specialists. We make deliberate efforts to ensure that they validly apply to two or more natural cultures (and possibly folk concepts). If these scientific concepts engage the interest of a number of scholars over more than a few years, the concepts evolve, becoming less and less anchored in, and colored by, natural culture contexts. Two of the important qualities sought in scientific concepts are intersystem validity and lack of ambiguity. These concerns are not necessarily true of folk concepts, and never characterize the whole of a natural culture.

We have two major sets of terms for labeling some of these matters, folk–analytic (often associated with Bohannan [1963:12]), and emic–etic (associated primarily with Pike and Harris [Headland, Pike, and Harris 1990]).

It is my position that we need at least a tripartite distinction, encompassing (1) concepts that a natural culture has and discusses (folk concepts), (2) a set of the distinctions which are needed for an analysis of a local reality (emic concepts for some), and (3) a set of all the distinctions which have ever been needed for an analysis of local realities (etic concepts for nearly everybody).

Emic–etic is, by some, equated with the folk–analytic distinction (e.g., Harris 1999; cf. Lett 1987, 1990; Headland, Pike, and Harris 1990). I reject the proposition that the emic–etic distinction is synonymous with the folk–analytic/scientific one for it is a distortion of the meanings of the terms in linguistics. In phonology, for example, a phonemic analysis uses all, and only, those distinctive features which are used in the natural language to produce meaningful utterances. There is no evidence that native speakers are consciously aware of any distinctive features, nor is there any evidence that there is any natural culture which indulges in phonological analysis of our analytic, scientific sort.

Phonemic analysis is done by the analyst, not by the native, and is done with scientific concepts (such as stop, voiceless, rising tone, etc.) and not with folk concepts. Phonemic analysis in linguistics produces an analysis of structure in the utterances of a natural language, but it does not use folk concepts to do it. It uses scientific concepts every step of the way. Therefore, although many colleagues equate emic–etic with folk–scientific, I reject that and will use only the contrast between folk and something else in this book.

Folk concepts occur in natural culture (and are referred to in natural language). They often are analytic in the partitioning sense. What they are not expected to do is achieve comparability across a number of natural cultures. Scientific concepts are expected to do exactly that. Therefore the opposition is not between folk and analytic but between two contexts for concepts, natural culture and scientific culture. I agree with Lett that these are above all statements in an epistemology, and that while there are "scientific" parts of some, perhaps all, natural cultures, science as a system is unlike any natural culture (Lett 1990).

I conclude that we need three names for three concepts: a name for the local concepts, and *folk concepts* seems the best candidate; a name for concepts used in the scientific analysis of the local reality, and *emic* seems a good candidate; and a name for the roster of concepts needed for an analysis of every local reality, and *etic* is a good candidate. A scientific anthropology needs to pay attention to all three.

Weak Version
The strong version of cultural contamination does not pose a problem for a scientific anthropology. The weak version of cultural contamination is serious and permanent. Any discipline that desires to operate in a transcultural context must come to grips with it.[6] The response in scientific anthropology to the problem of cultural contamination has been to develop scientific concepts which reduce or eliminate the assumptions and biases of any particular natural culture. A scientific concept may describe or contain several folk concepts, or it may describe some phenomena which are not even present in the folk concepts of a particular place.

As will become clear in part III, the problem of cultural contamination of the observation language has been recognized for many decades, and there have been serious efforts to deal with it. It has been, and remains, a serious challenge to comparability, and thus to a science of culture. Anthropologists have worked on constructing empirical observation languages which are not contaminated by the content of particular natural cultures, and we have achieved a large measure of success.

Ambiguity

A major challenge to comparability is ambiguity of the words used to represent the concepts. Science in the modern era (since at least Descartes) has stressed the importance of univocal instead of multivocal terms. Anthropologists have often remarked on the lack of unambiguous language in our field. Radcliffe-Brown noted in 1940 that

The choice of terms and their definitions is a matter of scientific convenience, but one of the characteristics of a science as soon as it has passed the first formative period is the existence of technical terms which are used in the same precise meaning by all the students of that science. By this test, I regret to say, social anthropology reveals itself as not yet a formed science. (Radcliffe-Brown 1940:3)

Others have noted the same difficulty with technical language in anthropology (Leach 1965:339; Kaplan and Manners 1972; Needham 1971a, 1975). One reason for this state of affairs is the influence of natural language.

Natural cultures (and their languages) have thousands of concepts, many of them named. But it is sometimes the case that a concept will be referred to with two or more names, and that each name will refer to two or more concepts. (Lakoff's discussion of prototypes in natural language is a good introduction [1987].)

Equality, equity, elitism, freedom, family values, choice, empowerment, and *responsibility* are words/names that are particularly salient (and particularly contested) in contemporary America. They all refer to more than a single concept, and each of the concepts has received at least two different names. It is possible to think, and write about, these matters keeping the various names and concepts clear (cf. Sen 1992 for a clear example on "inequality"). But it is far more likely that natural language discussions will *not* keep the names and concepts clearly separated.

If the discussion slips from one concept to another without marking it, if a keyword is used with one set of meanings in the first paragraph and with a different set of meanings in the last paragraph, then we do not have comparability of either the names or the concepts. When these conditions apply to the observation language we have a situation of high uncertainty. If the natural culture genius for ambiguity is allowed to dominate the discipline, then the comparability (and clarity) so necessary to science will be very difficult to achieve.

The condition all sciences strive for is that the concepts partition reality in valid ways, and that the concepts are named unambiguously. Science strives for a one-to-one-to-one relationship between partitions of reality, concepts, and names of concepts. The difference between the concept and name is easy to lose sight of. It takes very hard work to maintain the one-to-one relationship.

If we use a term to refer to only (and always) one concept, and if in our use we call a single concept by one name and one name only, we will have banished ambiguity and that constraint on comparability has been removed.

Constructing and maintaining such linguistic usages has been a scientific ideal for five hundred years in science.

But all such efforts are struggling against one of the most powerful forces of natural culture. We are all bathed by natural language almost all the time, and natural language, most of the time, encourages ambiguity. It is very difficult for any person, or any set of persons, to neutralize the forces which produce ambiguity.

It is thus clear that a major instance of a lack of one-to-one correspondence between concept and term occurs with "culture." I have opted for one of the horns of the ambiguity, and in addition have marked the term so that it is clear which concept I refer to when I use culture1.

Rodney Needham and others examined some concepts used in analysis of kinship in the ASA volume on kinship (Needham 1971a, 1971b; Rivière 1971) and found them hopelessly ambiguous. In 1975 Needham proposed that our discipline's terms are inherently ambiguous, and that they could best be described as family resemblance predicates. This latter notion comes from Ludwig Wittgenstein. It is a description of the semantics of some terms in natural language. The word *game* in English (the famous example) is applied to a wide variety of situations (it is modified by *baseball, chess, solitaire*, and *word*). There is no single criterion of meaning which is common to all these uses of the term, but most of the uses share some common criterion with at least one other use of the term. This example comes from natural language. Benson Saler has argued that the uses of *religion* in scholarly discourse form a family resemblance predicate, and that this is a necessary condition (Saler 1993).

And yet the prospect is not without hope. Natural language is not ambiguous everywhere. There are pools of expertise in natural languages where ambiguity seems to be reduced to a minimum, although we know relatively little about these pools. For example, I happen to be a party to the language used to describe the parts and operation of fore-and-aft-rigged sailboats in the United States. I learned it as a child, and have used it in most parts of the country. It is a specialized vocabulary, and it is usually portrayed as a useless (and mystifying) jargon by outsiders. The language is virtually without ambiguity and has been remarkably consistent across space (the lower forty-eight states) and over time (my lifetime).

There may be comparable phenomena among electricians, plumbers, structural steel workers, oil rig workers, and surgical theater teams. I would expect it wherever two or more people work on a job simultaneously, the environment of things and tasks is complex, at least some communication takes place in natural language, and there is some danger implied by imperfect communication. If I am right and these pools of descriptive language without ambiguity are systematic and shared in natural language, then ambiguity is not *the* condition of natural language but *one* condition. Therefore our species has a strong capacity to invent, use, and preserve descriptive languages that are virtually free of ambiguity, and there is reason to be optimistic about science.

Ambiguity in the language used to represent the observation concepts is a serious challenge to comparability. If one is persuaded that only natural languages exist, then the problem is nearly insuperable. But if one is persuaded that our species has been able to construct scientific cultures and languages, then the problem becomes manageable.

Conclusion

There are two major plausible challenges to comparability in a science of culture. There is the cultural contamination challenge to the existence of the same kinds of thing (both objects and dimensions), and there is the challenge to our capacity to eliminate or control ambiguity in how we name and discuss those things.

One view of the cultural world holds that natural cultures have different views of the world, and they are said to be incomparable. Every observer is embedded in a natural culture, and so their attempts at transcultural observation are hopelessly contaminated. Natural languages are the only languages one can use for observing phenomena, and since they differ, no transcultural comparability of observations is possible. The ambiguities so rife in natural languages make all natural languages inappropriate for naming transcultural things for science.

At the heart of these objections to comparability is the proposition that no stable "kinds of things," concepts or words, can apply in two or more cultures. The challenges facing a scientific cultural anthropology (and all social sciences) are then clear. A (social) science must have an observational language that identifies cross-culturally valid kinds of things, and it must have an observational language that does not suffer from ambiguity. Comparability of the observations demands that these conditions be met.

If the radical relativists are right about this matter, then no natural science of culture/human society is possible. If they are wrong, then there is hope for a scientific cultural anthropology. The rest of this book is an argument that they are wrong.

It is not widely known, but the natural sciences have had to solve these two problems, establishing valid kinds of things and unambiguous descriptive language. As we will see in part II, the solutions have been developing for thousands of years, are still developing, and have been successful. There are a small number of principles involved. Let us turn, then, to how these problems have been solved in natural scienc.

Notes

1. Two of the most fundamental terms in social science are *society* and *culture*. Virtually everybody treats at least one of them as a given in their analysis. If a culture exists, it is at least a reasonable question whether there is more than one of them. Everybody assumes so. If that is the case, then there must be some sort of boundary phenomena, otherwise there cannot be more than one of them. To the best of my knowledge nobody has shown us where the boundaries are, much less shown us why they think they know where the boundaries are. Society is often described as a system of social relationships. Can there be only one such system for all humans? If not, there are two or more. How does anyone know where the boundary is? There are almost no reports of empirical tests of the hypothesis that natural cultures are systems. Przeworski and Teune suggested one way to conduct such an empirical test (1970), but to my knowledge no one has conducted their test, or any other.

There are no clear positive answers to these questions for anthropologists. That is why I claim that society and culture are imputed, rather than found. If that is the case, the systemic nature, and integrity, of society and culture are assumed rather than found, therefore more than trivially uncertain, and therefore problematic.

2. Stating that a "culture" contains "concepts" of course reifies culture. Cultures do not have concepts, people do. But one of the uses of the culture concept is to capture what many of the members of that culture use as concepts. It is also summation and generalization.

3. The ambiguities in natural language ought to have profound effects upon the conclusions about perceptions and concepts. Winch did not deal with this problem. Donald Levine has begun to do so (1985).

4. A counterposition, that some meanings do not differ from culture to culture, is conceivable, and has often been used in psychological anthropology, particularly with respect to the Oedipus complex (see Spiro 1982).

5. The anthropology project that produces ethnographies (studies of a particular place) has been primarily motivated, since at least the days of Malinowski's teaching in London, to produce studies which privilege the differences, rather than the similarities, with other ethnographies (Keesing 1989). That it would be difficult to isolate similarities under these conditions is neither surprising nor defensible. The sciences of human behavior should be just as interested in what is common to human experiences as in what is rare or unique.

6. It will be interesting to see if art history and comparative literature, for example, recapitulate the long evolutionary experience of linguistics and anthropology as they grapple with the art and the literature of some very different "others." See Winter 2000 for a move in this direction.

PART II

COMPARABILITY IN NATURAL SCIENCE

In the preface it was claimed that apples and oranges can be compared. It is done by observing dimensions of the same kinds of objects. Two major challenges to comparability in observation languages have been identified, cultural contamination (or finding the same kinds of things), and ambiguity in the language we use. These problems apply both to the construction of scientific dimensions and to the construction of scientific objects. Part II is a consideration of how natural science has dealt with the two challenges to comparability for both dimensions and objects. Two dimensions are discussed, length and temperature. I then turn to a discussion of the more difficult subject of comparability among the objects. For both dimensions and objects we will see that there has been development of the observation languages and that development has included shifting from the language in a single natural culture to the attempt to construct a universal language. The most natural term to use here is universal. But universal could be taken to apply to the whole universe. We have no idea if our observational successes will apply elsewhere in the universe. In fact our success applies to the planet we live on, and probably to our solar system. Some of our observations apply elsewhere in the universe, but perhaps some of them do not. Therefore we should talk about an earthly language rather than a universal one.

CHAPTER THREE

~

Dimensions in Natural Science: Length and Temperature

It may well be the case that all human minds can operate with kinds of objects, and with attributes or characters or dimensions of objects. The natural cultures of the world suggest that it often occurs.

Explicit formal dimensions and objects are at least as old as markets. As soon as metal or cloth appeared in the market they would need to be identified as kinds of objects (gold, copper, obsidian, turquoise, wool, linen, etc.). Then the particular lot being sold (and bought) could be characterized as to the dimensions of number of pieces, size (extension, mass), quality, color, and so on. Finally, a price could be negotiated for the purchase and sale. Object and dimension is a highly plausible set of operations for any market exchange system.

Some folk cultures have invented dimensions that encompass a number of attributes in systematic ways. The marketplace seems to be a prime location for the operation (and perhaps invention) of systematic dimensional analysis. The dimensions we now call extension (length), mass (weight), and volume often had physical standards in marketplaces and were the subject of considerable official attention. They all occur early in the histories of old-world states. Price is another dimension which is characteristic of marketplaces.

Science, or at least science in modern Europe, has been vigorously and systematically inventing dimensions, and ways to observe them, that have planetary validity and acceptance. That effort has been successful. The vast bulk of our knowledge in natural science is based on the observation of attributes or dimensions of objects.[1] The mature physical sciences spend most of their time on dimensional analysis and relatively little time on the objects that manifest those dimensions.

The development of dimensions is slow, especially where we do not start with dimensions already worked out for the marketplace. And where the dimension is, for example, the quality of a product, such as an onion, or wool, where no physical standard is possible, it has been harder to achieve.

The Dimension of Length[2]

Many scientific dimensions have their origin in one or more natural cultures (cf. Crump 1990). Concepts of length, mass, time, and volume are to be found in some way or other in many natural cultures. Some of these folk concepts, and their associated observation technologies, were gradually converted into scientific observation procedures under the control of that universalizing culture we call science.

The earliest direct evidence we have of coherent and conscious use of dimensions does not occur before writing, which is relatively recent in the human career. However, given the widespread analytic strategy of attributes of objects, and given the making of tools to a pattern (such as hand axes), it seems very likely that the users of these objects were using something like the dimensions of extension, mass, and pattern.

Among the earliest objects made by humans (that we know about) are stone tools in the Olduwan Industrial Complex (Ambrose 2001:1749). Found over much of Africa, they were made to a very few patterns for nearly a million years starting about 2.5 million years ago (mya). About a million years later, large cutting tools such as hand axes, cleavers, picks, and knives (10 to 17 cm) are added, becoming part of the Acheulean Industrial Complex (Ambrose 2001:1750). These large cutting tools were made for about another million years.

It seems inevitable that humans as makers of things would be aware of, and able to consciously control decisions about, length. Hand axes are made to a pattern, but they are also made to size. Spears, arrows, bows, and projectile points all show a coherent intentionality about length. These homogeneities with respect to length are obviously related to the effective use of the object. A hand axe that measured two meters by two meters by thirty centimeters (2m x 2m x 30cm) would be impossible to use without substantial ways to amplify human muscle power. A hand ax 2mm x 2mm x 1mm would have few, if any, uses. The same holds for all utilitarian built objects.

The choice of length, then, was likely a function of the constraints of the human body and the materials worked with.

It is not necessary to assume that at the beginning there were shared concepts of length, nor that the dimension of length was divided into a standard segment. It is plausible to imagine that different early makers of large cutting tools could have used quite different units of length (equivalent to our inches and centimeters), each of which produced a tool of about the same size. If we assume that the maker and the user of the object are the same person, there would be little reason for shared understandings. Once exchange becomes widespread, however, shared understandings of such dimensions as length would likely become common, and perhaps necessary.

It seems likely that some other dimensions were also conceived very early, with kind of stone, mass, and temperature among the likely candidates. The early discovery and use of dimensions in human cognition and practice seem highly likely. Arriving at local agreement on such matters probably requires language and exchange. By the time we have direct evidence of natural culture measuring systems, with the written records of the third millennium BCE, there are systems of measurement present, involving dimensions of length, mass, and volume (Powell 1989, 1990).[3]

Comparability within a natural culture observation system was likely not a problem at the beginning. Even the invention of a common local tradition does not seem that problematic. It is when one tries to bridge natural culture systems that comparability certainly becomes problematic.[4]

Exchange within states will bring the problem of comparability to the surface of consciousness. States normally contain several natural cultures (included by immigration, conquest, or invasion), and so a state usually contains a number of natural culture measures. These different measuring systems are a direct and inescapable challenge to comparability.

There are a plethora of measurement standards within early modern states in Europe. Between the collapse of the Roman Empire and the rise of Napoleon, measures for volume, weight, and length in Europe varied from town to town, from industry to industry, from commodity to commodity, and from time to time. The situation in early modern Europe is particularly well documented, as the variety of measures was well known, and problematic to at least scholars and scientists.

In Holland in the sixteenth and seventeenth centuries, the term *roeda* referred to a unit of length. Lengths varied from the Hondsbosse roeda (north of the Ij) at 3.108 meters to the Stadsroeda in Groningen at 4.091 meters. The Hollandense *mijl* was 2,000 Rignlandse roeda of 3.767 meters (de Vries

1974:281–283). As for areas of land, there were many of them. The Rignlandse *morgen* was 600 square Rignlandse roeden (0.85 ha), and the Hondsbosse morgen was 800 square Hondsbosse roeden (0.98 ha) (de Vries
1974:281–283).

In Italy between the ninth and eighteenth centuries, the measures of almost everything differed from place to place, from time to time, and by what
was being measured. The sizes of the measures with the same names varied
from one place to another. Thus, the *piede* (foot) varied from Cannara at
0.223 meters to Cervia at 0.649 meters, and at Gubbio there was piede for
shipbuilding at 0.322 meters (Zupko 1981:152–154). The *miglio*, a length for
road and sea distances, was a descendant of the Roman mile of 8 *stadii* of
1,000 paces (0.481 km). At Milan before 1803 the miglio was equal to 1.785
kilometers, and after 1803 it was made equal to 1.0 kilometers. At Palermo
it was 1.487 kilometers, and at Cagliari it was 2.519 kilometers (Zupko
1981:152–154). The *mina* is a unit of area and of capacity. At Gubbio it was
0.333 hectares, whereas at Perugia it was 0.446 hectares. In Milan before
1803 it was 0.091 hectoliters, and after 1803 it was 0.100 hectoliters (Zupko
1981:156).

As can easily be seen, when there is a single name (roeda, miglio/mijl,
mina) used to refer to quite different standard units, there is substantial ambiguity in the naming of the unit of the dimension. Unless the unit is pref-
aced with the name (and date!) of the territory (e.g., the mina of Perugia, or
the mina of Milan), the resulting measure is ambiguous and therefore highly
uncertain.[5]

The effect of these differences is to make comparability extremely difficult. Even though the same names were used, these names had different values. For valid comparison to take place, the observer would have to know
that the names did not have the same meaning, and would furthermore have
to know the detailed meaning of the several instances of the same "word."

Alder, in his account of the precipitation of the metric system during the
1790s in France, describes a "just-price" economy that relied on a multiplic-
ity of measures (Alder 2002:132–134). According to Alder, towns had marketplaces but did not use a market principle. The price of a loaf of bread was
supposed to stay the same, the amount of flour in the bread was supposed to
be enough to feed someone, and to allow the baker to stay in business. When
flour was more expensive, the size of the loaf would be diminished, rather
than keep the amount of flour stable and raise the price. Apparently raising
the price of bread could lead to riots. In consequence, then, the authorities
controlled the price of bread (it was, in effect, a command economy so far as
price at the local retail level was concerned) and ignored changes in the size

of the loaf of bread. Linklater argues that weights and measures were under the control of local authorities, who were opposed to any national attempt to standardize them (2002:21–25)

Considerable efforts have been made by states to establish statewide standards for some of their dimensions (usually mass, volume, and length, and perhaps time). The first evidence we have of deliberate efforts to achieve cross-cultural comparability, then, is probably when the state declared standards of measurement.

Egypt and Mesopotamia both invented standards for the dimension of length. In the early dynasties of Egypt the cubit was the standard unit of length for architecture and other midrange phenomena. The cubit was supposed to be the length of the pharaoh's forearm, from tip of the longest finger to the elbow. This was divided into six palms or hands, about the width of the hand. These again were divided into four lengths about the width of a finger. The values on this dimension were represented by numbers: the height of an object could be described as four cubits, three palms, and one finger (Kendall 1986). In Mesopotamia the same central specification held. One of the statues of Gudea, a ruler of Lagash, has the king holding a model of a standard of length on his lap (Gudea B [in the Louvre]).

Therefore, no systematic comparison of lengths from one reign to another can be done without knowing what the standard was for each reign. Many of the agrarian states in the ancient Near East had a concept of length, but even when they used the same name for the unit (cubit) they had different standards.

The incentive on the part of the state both to impose a single set of measures and to maintain the stability (honesty) of those measures is strong. Part of this no doubt stems from the responsibility of the state to establish measurement standards for the market (Linklater 2002:25–28).

At the same time, the incentive to use different measures is also strong. Those selling a commodity have an incentive to use measures of standard name but substandard capacity (volume or mass). Those being taxed on a commodity have an incentive to use a smaller measure than the standard and thus to pay less tax. The state has an incentive to issue debased coins (either less weight, or diluted with base metal), in order to preserve state wealth. In the world of the exchange of goods, it is clear why caveat emptor is the cardinal rule.

Why would the state want to establish standards for weights and measures, when there are incentives to not have them? Some suggestions may be offered. Artisans and merchants who operated in more than one market or region would need to compare amounts of things (as well as quality), and the relationship of amount to price must be a prime consideration. A single standard for weights and measures would simplify the calculations. On the other hand, perhaps merchants (as well as moneylenders) were able to learn and operate the various measurement standards, and it might well have been to their advantage to have multiple measuring systems.

Another possible motivation might be tax collections by the center. A central authority would have some advantage if a single standard were always in use, for it would save the center the effort of learning, calculating, and validating the multiple heaps of grain and so forth that were collected as tax.

One more motivation is that of justice. Agrarian states usually claim legitimacy in part because of their administration of justice. Honest weights and measures seem to play a significant role in this rhetoric. One can easily imagine that the "peace of the market"[6] is enhanced by authoritative, and public, standards. If there is a dispute over a transaction due to different calculations of amount, the authoritative standards will resolve the issue.[7]

The state can declare a standard. Whether the state can force the population to use only that standard is another question, and one that begs for investigation. Presumably the state is more interested in standardizing weights and measures synchronically over a territory, and has less interest in standardization over long periods of time. By this analysis the interest of the state is in commerce, taxation, and perhaps construction, and these will be concerns of the moment, not for all time.

The principal force for differentiation across time is semantic drift. Semantic drift is a major source of ambiguity in the dimensions, names of dimensions, and objects in natural cultures, especially after the breakup of an empire. There is a strong tendency for many phenomena in language to change slowly. There is always pressure for slow change in the sound system, in the grammar system, in the lexical system, and in the meaning system. Semantic drift works its way on the words of language in what might be called a glacial process. It is slow, usually so slow that most people are not aware of the change, and it is very powerful. Part of this semantic drift is the independent shifting of concepts and words, the constant creation (and destruction) of ambiguity. It is highly likely that the various local measures in Europe are in part the result of drift from Roman standards in Italy. There are sources of variation other than drift. The control of an empire may not eliminate the previous local measures. When an empire, or at least its attempts at standardizing weights and measures, fades, the underlying regional standards may once again flourish, this time "contaminated" in some ways by the previous imperial standards. Another source is different standards imported by immigrants, either peaceful or conquering. Semantic drift is universal to natural language. It takes great effort to try to hold language constant in time and place, and it is very difficult to achieve. The most that can be done is to slow the rate of change by a very considerable amount. Efforts to stop, or at least slow to a crawl, this kind of change are widely noticed, if not very prevalent. The French Academy's attempts to control change in the French language is one major example.

The control over semantic drift requires several areas of agreement. There must be an agreement that core vocabulary and core concepts exist, the definitions must be established in such a way that a substantial number of important and powerful participants can agree, and then the use of these concepts in ordinary transactions must conform to these definitions.[8]

States have often attempted to define, and impose, standards for dimensions, and have often failed. Powell (1989, 1990) has analyzed the system of measures in the ancient Near East, and shows it to have been a remarkably simple and coherent system in design. There is no evidence that it lasted any substantial period of time (a victim of, among other things, semantic drift). Adams demonstrated that the thirteenth-century English system of weights and measures was simple and coherent, and that most of the dimensions and units drifted, as a consequence (in part) of parliamentary decisions (Adams 1821). The old basic words for dimensions came to have radically different new meanings.

Universal Comparability—The Metric System

The most stable, successful, and widespread system of empirical observation language is what is commonly called the metric system. It was promoted by the revolutionary parliament in France, constructed by eminent scientists, and has since become the standard of international measurement. All science and almost all manufacturing and commerce now take place in metric dimensions. If the interests of markets and the state are relatively synchronic, the interests of scientists are decidedly diachronic as well. Scientists want measures to be comparable across time as well as across space.

Prior to 1790 virtually all attempts to establish statewide systems of weights and measures were piecemeal, and probably not very effective. They were also unicentric efforts, limited to the territory of sovereignty of that particular state. The metric system is a single coherent system of fundamental dimensions, it was constructed by scientists, and its successor, SI[9] (International System of Units), is supported by commercial interests, manufacturing interests, science, states, and international treaties. What is so different about SI is the degree of consensus that has been built around it, and that is largely a social phenomenon, not a technical one. SI is socially constructed, but it is not socially constructed by a single natural culture.

Immediately after the Revolution, the French attempted radical reforms of three systems of measurement—the calendar, the clock, and weights and measures. The first two were in effect stillborn, and are today only curiosities. Large parts of the third, weights and measures, did become the standard for France, soon thereafter for most of continental Europe, and later for the rest of the world.

Talleyrand in the Assembly organized the task for the Academy of Sciences. The Academy in turn appointed a ". . . committee to formulate a practical program for fundamental reform of weights and measures for all France" (Klein 1974:108). The committee included Condorcet, Lagrange, and Laplace. In addition, Lavoisier was involved until his death upon the guillotine. Internationally eminent French scientists were asked by a state to generate a new, simple, and standardized set of weights and measures. They were successful.

One of their decisions was the numerical base, and after much discussion they chose base 10, or the decimal form.[10] Then they decided that the unit of length would be used to derive area and volume. Finally, basic weight would be derived from a volume of pure water. Their choice for the standard for the unit of length was 1/10,000,000 part of a quadrant (from equator to pole) of the earth's circumference. The gram was defined as the weight of pure water at 4 degrees Celsius that occupied one cubic centimeter.[11] (The volume of liquid water is smallest at 4 degrees Celsius.) The system was a single system, based on a small number of fundamental dimensions based on natural constants. The base 10 choice permits mathematical manipulation more easily than does the usual doubling system.

The committee's proposals to the Constituent Assembly were accepted in 1791 (Klein 1974:112). In 1798, European scientists were invited to France to help perfect the system. The English-speaking nations of Great Britain and the newly fledged United States of America declined to attend. The various committees prepared new standards for the meter and the gram. The meter was now represented by the distance between two lines on a platinum bar, and the kilogram was a cylinder made of platinum. In 1799 the French Parliament ratified the new standards, and eventually the system spread to Switzerland, Italy, and parts of Germany (Zupko 1990). The Netherlands and Belgium adopted the metric system when occupied by Napoleon.

The metric system became official in 1799 in France, but there were provisions in the legislation that permitted the older popular measures to remain in use. It was not until 1837 that France abolished the nonmetric units (Klein 1974:125).

From the very beginning there was a merger of scientific, commercial, and political interests. The French Revolution adopted the metric system as one official set of weights and standards for the French Republic, and so they applied equally to commerce and manufacturing, and to scientific endeavors. Length was conceived of as a dimension, and it was based on a unit, the meter, that was at the scale of the human body.

Soon after the Treaty of Versailles (1815) there was a movement to establish an international treaty on matters of measurement. Whereas before it was up to the central bureaucracy of each state to invent and impose a single measurement system, now there was a multicentric (although at the beginning only in Europe) movement to accomplish the same thing, but without political power. An International Treaty of the Meter was first signed in 1875, with thirty nations in attendance (Zupko 1990:228). After 1875, other nations gradually accepted the metric standards as legal.

In the early part of the nineteenth century Great Britain also underwent a reform of weights and measures, culminating in a massive reform in 1824 (Zupko 1990). The United Kingdom adopted a single set of standards for weights and measures, which incidentally explains why the United States, descended from England, has the same words for weights and measures but often uses different values for them. The United States made the metric system legal in 1866, signed the Treaty of the Meter in 1875, received copies of the standard meter and kilogram in 1890, and three years later redefined the customary units in metric terms (Chisholm 2002).[12] In the United States we continue to use the customary units, but they are now defined in terms of the SI system. The United States has not replaced the U.S. customary units in public use with the metric ones.

There are now periodic conferences to discuss the concepts (which include the standards) and the meanings of the words used in measuring, and virtually all nations of the world now participate. There is still a joining of the commercial and scientific worlds in this convention. The General Conference on Weights and Measures (Conférence Général des Poids et Mesures) publishes its results, and there are hundreds of handbooks available which define the various units. Every major nation has a bureau of weights and standards which is supposed to calibrate and standardize the measuring instruments in that nation (in the United States it is now called the National Institute of Standards and Technology [NIST]). This again includes the scientific, manufacturing, and commercial spheres of action.

The conference establishes a concept for a dimension (extension), one word with a single definition for the basic unit of the dimension (meter), and a single operation that establishes the basic unit. Furthermore, periodic conventions meet to decide on matters of dimensions, their concepts, and their names, and these conventions make decisions on these matters. The decisions are adhered to by vast numbers of users.

The early agrarian states then certainly contained the concept of a dimension of (some kinds of) objects, in this case length. It was in some places a general concept, divorced from particular instances of it. By the attempt to define a standard for the dimension, they attempted to achieve comparability.

The Problem of Cultural Contamination

One of the two principal challenges to comparability is cultural contamination. If the arena of action is a single culture, then cultural contamination may not be problematic. A problem arises when there is an attempt to acquire or compare measures in two or more different cultures. This difficulty occurs automatically in trade between two cultures.

The agrarian state solved the problem for length by using a nearly arbitrary standard. The cubit was the standard of length for much of the Mediterranean world. The Romans used the stride (by which they meant a double stride, the distance between the placements of the right foot when walking at a normal pace). These standards are imprecise, in that the "natural" basis for them is significantly variable. But as long as *some* standard was set, then the state could live with the result.

The better way to establish a planetary meaning for the unit of length is to define it in terms of a natural constant, an invariant natural event or structure, rather than a variable one (such as the length of this person's stride, or the length of that pharaoh's forearm). The solution is a definition immune to the several meanings promoted by local natural cultures. The French developed a measurement system which was designed to be independent of the many local measures precisely by being anchored in what were then thought to be planetary natural constants.

The natural constant for length was to be the circumference of the earth. The basic unit of length, the meter, was defined as 1/10,000,000 of one quarter of the circumference of the earth (the earth was assumed to be a perfect sphere). As a consequence, theoretically the standard of length could be calibrated anywhere on the surface of the earth with the proper equipment. The standard did not have to be transported from somewhere else. In fact such calibrations were expensive and difficult. The attempt to measure the length of the quadrant (from Dunkirk to Barcelona, passing through Paris) did not produce a definitive result. Instead a standard bar of platinum in the vault at Sèvres was established as the standard, with large numbers of exact copies distributed widely (Alder 2002).

By this stroke the fundamental unit was based on what was then thought to be a constant universal natural fact (universal at least as far as this planet is concerned) and thereby escaped from the multiple worlds of natural cultures. It is thereby exempt from cultural contamination, both in definition and in use. Any natural cultural concept of length can be related to this universal form by means of empirical analysis and transform rules.

Another way to achieve comparability of the observation concept is to manufacture and disseminate devices which reproduce the standard. Length is often measured with such a device, a ruler. The use of the device is relatively simple, and needs experience but little training. The making of the device is not necessarily a simple task, and it must be done with great attention paid to validity and reliability. But the devices themselves are now mass-produced and widely available. One does not have to be an expert on the metric system to use a tape measure marked off in meters. The measurements taken with the device are subject to operator error, but not to cultural contamination.

The advantage of this system for science could not be greater. Instead of a wild variety of local systems of measuring things, with no common base, now there was a single, simple, easily calibrated system which linked length, volume, and area together as one set. Furthermore, the base number system was common to them all, and was the easily manipulated decimal system. With this system, measurement in natural science became far more convenient. Communication of the results of measurement across language and cultural boundaries become much less of a problem, as a major source of uncertainty was removed.

The Problem of Ambiguity

Within science there may be fewer sources of semantic drift than there are in commerce. It seems that the interest in cheating on the weights and measures is weaker (than in commerce) due to the privileging of public results and replication. Communication of results is vastly enhanced if they are comparable. And most natural scientists are powerfully interested in expanding their reputations, which is achieved in no small part by having other scientists become aware of, understand, and accept, rather than reject, their results. This process is enhanced by using a standardized observation language.

Another force possibly promoting semantic drift is a major drive in science, discovery. Discovery rewards individualism. Individualism should pose problems for the enforcement of a set of meanings for terms, some of which (at any point in time) are not very productively defined. There is a problem of social control here which must be solved, and indeed is solved. It may be a measure of the maturity of a discipline that it is able to establish and abide by the results of conferences on terminology.[13]

A third force promoting semantic drift is the multinational nature of science. There are physicists, molecular biologists, and taxonomists working in Chinese, Russian, Arabic, Hindi, English, French, Spanish, Italian, German, and probably many other natural languages. To the degree that any of these groups are relatively isolated, their observation concepts will be prone to drift. The use of a single prose language as the principal one of science (Latin, Arabic, German, now English) helps to reduce the drift, as undoubtedly do international conferences and international circulation of scientific journals. But the existence of a single, standardized empirical observation language is a major contributor to comparability across these natural language boundaries.

The state on occasion tries to use bureaucracy and force to control semantic drift in systems of weights and measures. It requires constant attention, and is not always effective. In modern society the enforcement mechanisms have become virtually invisible to ordinary citizens, but they exist and continue to operate.

In science there are some institutions to control the drift. Semantic drift is now controlled by international conferences which are empowered by members of the discipline to establish meanings for basic terms for the whole discipline. Embedded in the International Treaty of the Meter is an International Committee on Weights and Measures, and periodically a Conference on Weights and Measures. Changes in the definitions of terms must be approved by the conference. The conference, then, acts to prevent semantic drift and control semantic change.

The SI system now has control over ambiguity in the empirical observation language. It is accomplished by voluntary participation in a social structure. It is a monumental cultural achievement, one that has not been recognized widely enough. There are many other areas of commerce, manufacturing, and science where such conferences take place (e.g., international unions, international marine organizations).

Development of Length in SI

At the time of the French Revolution there was a political creation of a single theoretical measurement system out of a previous measurement anarchy. But the story did not stop there. Many of the attributes of the empirical observation language have continued to change.

The theoretical observation language had to be operationalized by empirically determining the length of the meter. The first effort to empirically measure the meter, a surveying trip from Dunkirk to Barcelona from 1792 to 1799, measured the length of 10° of latitude (1/9th of a quadrant) and was supposed to be able to determine empirically a standard for the meter (see Alder 2002). All other operations were arithmetical (adding, subtracting, multiplying, dividing).

Investigation of the basic standard, how it is defined, and how it is measured has continued and will continue. It was already clear in 1799 that the earth was not a perfect sphere, and so where on a quadrant one made the observation of the standard mattered. As the nineteenth century geological revolution showed, it could not be assumed that the shape of the surface of the earth was a constant. By the mid-twentieth century the basic definition of the meter switched to radiation rather than the circumference of the earth. It is now thought that radiation is a more stable constant than the shape of our planet. In 1960 a new definition of the meter was adopted in a meeting of the Treaty of the Meter nations: "The meter is the length equal to 1,650,763.73 wavelengths in vacuum of the radiation corresponding to the transition between the levels 2p15 of the Krypton-86 atom" (Klein 1974:187). In 1983 another new standard was accepted: ". . . the distance light travels in a vacuum in a time of 1/299,792,459 of a second (0.0000003 second) . . ." (Darton and Clark 1994:270).

In addition to the concern with the constant, there has also been a concern with precision, the number of subdivisions of the basic unit. The technology to produce an observation of 1/299,792,459 of a second did not exist in 1799. With the development of observation technology and theoretical understanding, the small ends of the scales of fundamental dimensions (extension, time, mass, temperature) have gained in importance (see Flowers 2004 for a summary account). There is no reason to expect the SI system to stop developing. The point is that many parties have agreed on how the system is to change.

The concept of a dimension of length has not developed, but the standard for calibration of that dimension has continued to improve. It makes perfect sense that our definition of a particular length would improve. Our understanding of micro and macro features of nature has improved, both because of theory and because of the advances in technology for observation (microscopes, telescopes). For our descriptions and explanations to continue to improve, our ability to observe must continue to improve (and vice versa). One cannot for long advance without the other. We are then involved in a developmental process which is of very long duration.

The Dimension of Temperature

Temperature as a dimension has a history that is interesting for several reasons. It had been used for production millennia before it was measured with a device. A practical thermometer was achieved considerably before an understanding of thermodynamic processes. It is a reactive measure. It is measured indirectly. And some scales have negative numbers. It is therefore more closely allied with many dimensions of human behavior (including cultural ones) than is length.

Temperature differences must have been readily observable, and used, very early on. Fever is a good indicator of illness, and the differences in human body temperature associated with fever, "normal life," and death could not have escaped human notice. Once fire came under human control surely the cooking of food cannot have been much later. Cultures with pottery, metal, and glass had to produce, sustain, and manage temperatures substantially higher than anything involving cooking food. Perceptions of the heat of the fire can be obtained by skin sensations, and in some cases visually. There must have been folk knowledge of temperature differences and amounts, generated by the health versus infection, and the need to manage cooking, the kiln, and the furnace.

Temperature was observed with a device very late in the game. Extension, volume, and mass were represented with objects (and standard objects) by the third millennium BCE. It seems likely that these were operating in exchange (perhaps even in marketplaces), whereas control over temperature was necessary only in production. There was likely some benefit in keeping knowledge of controlling temperature in manufacturing secret, or at least confined to one's workshop. The market, always involving exchange between at least two parties, seemingly evolved public standards much earlier.

There were a number of knotty problems to be solved in the case of temperature. The concept of extension (or length) is quite simple at the scale of human life, and understanding it involves little more than perceptual ability. Although very small and very large distances are extremely challenging to measure, and require an understanding of atoms and space-time, distances on and around our planet that are perceived by humans are simple in concept.

Temperature is much more complex. Theoretical understanding of the structure of matter (atomic structure, thermodynamics) eventually resulted in a concept of thermodynamic temperature. It covers the entire range of possible temperatures in the universe, from absolute zero, which is the absence of heat, to the extreme heat of the big bang. To this day the extremes are easier to conceptualize than to measure.

Measuring the temperature of some particular object, on the other hand, is done with a practical thermometer scale and device. Every device used to measure temperature is limited in the range of thermodynamic temperature it can cover, and no device is perfect for the task. Early practical devices focused on the temperature range of human life, and quickly worked their way below the freezing point of water and up to the boiling point of water. This came before an accepted general understanding of thermodynamics (with William Thompson, Lord Kelvin in 1848).

Practical (or empirical) thermometry with a device started around 1600 CE. The early solutions to the problem used the expansion and contraction of a liquid in glass tubes as the indicator of differences in temperature. Problems to be solved included identifying the liquids and their behavior, the container for the liquid, calibration of the instruments, the scale to be used, differences in the behavior of the objects being measured for temperature (gas, liquid, solid), and the nature of heat.

Galileo is among those credited with the first device to show differences in temperature (Middleton 1966). It consisted of a basin containing a liquid, and in the liquid was suspended a small tube. If the contents of the bowl became warmer, the liquid in the basin expanded, and the liquid would rise in the tube. Two natural phenomena were of great interest—the temperature differences in the human body (particularly those associated with illness) and the temperature of the air.

Over the next century there was widespread and intense interest in achieving the measurement of temperature in western Europe. Major centers of work were found in Florence, England, France, and Holland. The range of temperatures measured expanded, down to the freezing point of mercury (−38.84°C) and up to the boiling point of sulphur (444°C).

A liquid was the obvious choice of a substance to respond to differences in heat, for the liquids are visible or can be made so (unlike ordinary air), and the contraction and expansion are sufficiently large to be seen by the unaided eye. Water was the first choice. Two other choices were quickly considered—alcohol and mercury. Both were superior to water as they did not become solid at the freezing point of water. Both presented problems (of evaporation of alcohol, and small expansion of mercury). They are still the two main choices for inexpensive thermometers. As work progressed it became clear that the evaporation of alcohol was a problem, and that mercury and alcohol did not respond in exactly the same way (Middleton 1966:116, 124–126).

The obvious choice of substance for a container of the liquid was glass. It is transparent, and so the change in the position of the liquid inside was obvious. It was assumed at the beginning that the behavior of the glass was not a factor, and later this turned out to be a false assumption. Crystal (with lead) was inferior to pure glass, and some kinds of glass are not dimensionally stable over time (Middleton 1966:145–147).

Another issue was the design of the container. At the beginning the thermometers were open to the atmosphere. This allowed for expansion/contraction of the index substance, but also meant that the behavior of the liquid was affected by atmospheric pressure as well as by heat. The Grand Duke Ferdinand II in Florence solved this problem by sealing the device in about 1654 (Middleton 1966:28).

A problem from the beginning was how to calibrate different thermometers to each other. The solution was to anchor the measurement of temperature in some phenomenon of nature. Two were used at the beginning—the phase-shift of water between solid and liquid (either the freezing point of water or the melting point of ice) and the temperature of a "healthy human body." It is not immediately obvious why these anchor points were regarded as constants, as in fact they are not. The temperature of the human body varies from person to person and from time to time. The temperature at which water freezes or boils varies with atmospheric pressure and the substances dissolved in the water. It may be the case that the variations for each of these was too small to be perceived by any prethermometer means, and that for all practical purposes, then, the anchor points could be treated as constants. With greater precision in measuring temperature, the variations would become obvious, and finding the anchor points became a more important and demanding task.

Another anchor point quickly became of interest: the lowest temperature of a mixture of ice, water, and salt ($-17.8°C$, $0°F$, considerably lower than the freezing point). Eventually, another phase shift of water, the liquid-gas one (the boiling point of water), was included, although it was more problematic because it was strongly affected by air pressure. The scientific world eventually settled on the two phase shifts of distilled water at one atmosphere of pressure as the fixed points for a temperature scale (Middleton 1966).

A thermoscope, as invented by Galileo, displayed differences in temperature. But if measurement was desired, a scale for those differences was necessary, and many were developed. Scales proliferated as different scientists and instrument makers struggled with the task. One thermometer (from as late as 1841) was equipped with eighteen different temperature scales (Middleton 1966:65–66). As control over the instruments developed, so did the precision of measurements and the desire for precision. The divisions of the scales accordingly increased. Florentine thermometers of the mid-seventeenth century were made with three scales: fifty degrees, one hundred degrees, and one with three hundred degrees (Middleton 1966:34). The major scale in France was by Reaumur, with eighty degrees between freezing and boiling. The major scale in England was by Fahrenheit, with one hundred eighty degrees between freezing and boiling. Both were replaced by the Celsius scale, with one hundred degrees between the two points, and this became the temperature scale for the metric system. All these scales had a zero (0) in the range of life on earth, so all had negative numbers.

The contributions of Celsius (also an astronomer) were to set the fixed points at the boiling and freezing of water and to use a scale of one hundred equal intervals. Celsius set zero at boiling and one hundred at freezing, and later scientists and instrument makers reversed it (Klein 1974:312–315). The advantage of a scale of one hundred equal units is that it is easily handled in arithmetic terms.

The basic unit of length (cubit, foot, meter) has been named with a word for millennia. The way to assign a name to the length of an object has been a number, the number of the basic units manifested in the object. This makes the name unambiguous because of the uniqueness property of natural numbers. It is inherently the case that each natural number is unique. A 2 is always, and only, 2. It is never 3, or 20, or 22. An extremely large set of natural numbers can easily be named (in many but not all natural languages) without ambiguity. The basic unit has to be named in words (inch, meter, cubit), but the examples of it are unambiguously named with numbers.

Not only do numbers have many interesting properties, but so do the scale types in which numbers are embedded. The scales for measuring temperature established by Fahrenheit, Reaumur, and Celsius have a very interesting property, and one that is not often appreciated or understood. All of these scales set a zero point somewhere in the middle. There was no concept of an absence of temperature. Zero degrees was set at some fixed point in nature (such as the freezing point of water, or the coldest water one could achieve). Negative numbers were therefore possible.

The psychologist Stevens in 1946 argued that there are four basic scale types, all based on properties of numbers. More important, he argued that the interpretive mathematics we can use on scales varies significantly from one scale type to another. Length is measured with a ratio scale. It has a true zero,[14] it has equal intervals, and the numbers have uniqueness. An equal-interval scale is based on the equal-interval property of natural numbers: that is, $100 - 99 = 1$, and $4 - 3 = 1$, so that the difference between 100 and 99 is equal to the difference between 4 and 3 ($100 - 99 = 4 - 3$). Furthermore, this equality of interval is found over the entire range of the scale. It should be clear, then, that the linearity of response of the index substance is crucial. If mercury or alcohol do not respond in linear ways as their heat is changed from 0°C to 100°C, then we do not have an (equal) interval scale.

The interval scale for human behavior we are most likely to hear about in our daily life is the IQ. Here the scale value of one hundred is set at the mean of the population. With a center value greater than zero, it is fairly easy to assume that there is a zero value (for IQ.) In fact, no such concept yet exists. The reason for searching for it is to analyze the results of IQ observations with more powerful mathematical tools than are legitimately used with interval scales. IQ is also measured indirectly, and the linearity of the scale is in doubt towards the ends of the distribution.

In the case of temperature it was easy enough to conceive of equal intervals (length and mass were before us as an example). They are harder to operationalize, and in some respects we have still not achieved them, given the nonlinear behavior of our temperature measuring devices.

Temperature scales were originally equal interval, and only later did they become ratio scales. It took another century and a half to achieve a fundamental understanding of the underlying phenomena and to generate a scale for temperature that is a ratio scale, with a true zero, the Kelvin scale. The basic unit is still one degree Celsius, but the zero point has been set at 0 Kelvin, or –273.15°C. This is possible due to an understanding of the absence of kinetic energy in molecules.

The original thermoscopes, and thermometers, were open to the air. They were first closed off in the middle of the seventeenth century in Florence, which had a very large consequence. The substance used to measure heat is one that expands and contracts with differences in heat. But another cause of expansion and contraction is variation in atmospheric pressure. If the thermometer is open to the air, then both pressure and heat are operating simultaneously. Closing the measuring device removes one of the causes. (Barometers—devices used to measure differences in air pressure—were developed at the same time; see Middleton 1964.)

What happened is an important aspect of the reduction of ambiguity. If an observational technology systematically conflates two or more phenomena, then the observations recorded inevitably confuse our understanding of the phenomena. In order to maximize comparability we need dimensions that are monothetic, that are based on only one component, not two or more.

Monothetic refers to the condition that only a single dimension is involved. Before thermometer tubes were closed, the device measured the effects of temperature and air pressure simultaneously. The device was not measuring a monothetic dimension. Once the tube was closed, then air pressure was removed as a source of variation, and the dimension (as represented by the device) took a giant leap towards being monothetic.

Our scientific understanding of the empirical world is increased by our success in finding monothetic dimensions. It is vastly increased if we can find fundamental dimensions, and then combine those in clear ways (velocity, for example, needs observations on two fundamental dimensions, length and time.) Finding monothetic dimensions in social science has been a long, arduous, and difficult process. The reason for trying to do it is not physics envy but the need to find single kinds of things and thereby improve the quality of observations and subsequent analyses.

Temperature is measured indirectly. We have here a very different phenomenon from our example of length. Length is perceived, and measured, directly (at least in the range of the human body). In the case of temperature we have only indirect measurement. To explain this issue we must first deal with the theoretical understanding of heat and temperature. Although Amontons suggested a molecular basis for temperature, most used the hypothetical existence of a substance (caloric) as the source of heat. Heat was supposed to be caused by caloric, which was thought of as some kind of liquid. A rise in heat was caused by the addition of caloric, and a fall in heat was caused by the subtraction of caloric. After much searching, no evidence of the liquid was found, and other explanations became more effective. With hindsight we now see that the concept of caloric is unnecessary (Klein 1974:248–249).

Gains in theoretical understanding of matter led to a radically different view of heat by 1848. In this view, matter is composed of molecules and atoms, and each molecule or atom is in motion. Each molecule or atom has a short distance to travel. The average kinetic energy of each moving molecule or atom (the motion of the constituents of matter) is the fundamental concept of heat.

We are unable to directly observe the motion of molecules and atoms. The scale of the phenomena is (so far, at least) vastly smaller than the scale of the measurement technology. We must therefore find some indirect way to observe it. How we do that is explained by the laws of thermodynamics, which say that heat flows from a hotter body to a cooler, and not the other way around. If we can find substances that will react in a stable way to the flow of heat from one body to another, then we can compare and indirectly measure the differences in heat between two bodies (one being our measuring device). Our current understanding of heat is therefore a product of both generalizing theory and detailed understanding of the instruments that we use to measure temperature. Heat is the concept of average kinetic energy of molecules and atoms, and temperature is (one component of) the behavior of index substances that we use to indirectly measure differences in heat between two bodies.

Overdetermination, where more than one dimension or force is affecting the phenomena used as a measure of outcome, is a persistent problem with indirect measurement. If the phenomenon being used for indirect measurement (say, a column of mercury) is also being affected by other forces (friction, evaporation) at the time one is attempting to measure temperature, then the resultant measure is a combination of the forces and does not represent only the temperature.

Early thermometer instruments were responding to air pressure and to temperature. Once the instrument evolved, then air pressure was no longer conflated with temperature. Furthermore, with the invention of a device to measure air pressure (the barometer) they could start to measure the correlation of pressure with temperature. We have learned that the boiling point of water is not a constant, but is affected by atmospheric pressure. At higher altitudes (and therefore lower pressures), the boiling point of water is reduced. At altitudes lower than sea level (higher atmospheric pressure), the boiling point of water is increased. As a result, the phase shift points of water are now defined as being taken at one atmosphere of pressure.[15]

While air pressure has been removed from the measure of heat, we still have not removed the effects of nonlinear behavior of the substances used to absorb or lose heat. This nonlinear behavior compromises comparability. Mercury, alcohol, nitrogen gas, and other substances used in expansion tubes do not respond with perfect linearity. Consequently, the metrologist must constantly try to measure the influence of these other sources of variation and try to understand the theoretical foundation of the behavior. Indirect measurement is far more expensive, time-consuming, and error-prone than direct measurement.

A further problem with measuring temperature is that it can be a reactive measure. The issue is whether the act of measurement affects what is being measured. (This problem looms large in the observation of cultural phenomena.) When we are measuring the length of a box or a rice field, our use of measuring technology has no discernable effect on the box or the field. Our measures of stellar distance have no effect upon the distance of stellar objects.

It is not the same with liquid thermometers. The thermodynamic concept is that heat flows from a hotter body to a cooler one. This entails a thermal equilibrium. The measuring device contains heat and must arrive at the same temperature as the object being measured. The object being measured must therefore react to the heat of the liquid-in-glass thermometer, and the two must come to the "same" temperature. Therefore, the heat in the thermometer is affecting the heat in the object, and it is therefore a reactive measure. Furthermore, the measuring device must be observable, so in the usual case at least part of it must be outside the object. Therefore, the part outside must be in thermal equilibrium with its environment, which is usually not at the same temperature as the object.

In this case, the scale of the two objects matters. If a thermometer has a mass of one gram, and we are measuring an object (say, a lake) weighing millions of grams, the act of measuring will have no significant effect upon the temperature of the lake. But as the masses of the two objects approach each other, the mutual effects loom larger. It is clear that some attempts to observe may perturb the events (known as reactive measures). The perturbations can be observed, studied, and known, and it is possible to find ways of taking the disturbance into account.

There is another consideration. The index substances (mercury, alcohol) are chosen for their large and rapid changes in volume with changes in temperature. But they have to be contained in something, and that something must also arrive at thermal equilibrium. Glass has been the choice from the beginning, probably due originally to its transparency. But the glass, being solid, also expands far less than the liquids it contains.

We are still measuring temperature indirectly. And there is no single way to measure temperature over the entirety of the range. Strange nonlinear behavior is the rule below forty degrees Kelvin. And at temperatures above around two thousand degrees Kelvin, no substance is stable enough to use, so instead we use radiation phenomena as indices. The technology of temperature measurement is less successful than that for mass and length and can be expected to develop much more vigorously. Probably the basic definition of temperature will evolve to using radiation phenomena, just as length and time have. As of this writing, mass is the only fundamental physical dimension still defined in terms of an object, a platinum-iridium cylinder in a Paris vault (Kestenbaum 1998).

In the case of temperature we have a dimension that was measured with a device relatively late in natural cultures. The technology for measuring it also developed relatively late. And the underlying conception of the dimension is far less obvious to the intuitive eye. At the beginning of scientific measurement the primary interest was in temperatures of life. Water is basic to life, and the phase shift[16] temperatures of water are extremely handy for establishing fixed points. Since the measuring technology was a special device, not readily made by everybody, the standard for the basic unit was relatively easily disseminated, for it was contained in every thermometer.

Ambiguity in the language of recording was reduced by the use of numbers. But the simultaneous existence of several scales (Fahrenheit, Celsius,

Reaumur) meant that ambiguity was possible. From the beginning, every recorded temperature has had to indicate which scale was being used.

There is no evidence here that I can see for contamination of the measure of temperature by natural cultures. Ethnocentrism does not look to be part of the picture.

There was a great deal of development of understanding of the underlying phenomenon between 1600 and 1850, and in consequence the scientific community has settled on the Kelvin as the unit of temperature (same as the Celsius degree, one hundred of them between the two phase shifts of water). The technology for measuring temperature is still somewhat chaotic, especially over the very low and very high ranges.

The problem of ambiguity is solved by a monothetic dimension (average kinetic energy of molecules), a known scale type (interval at first, now ratio), use of numbers to describe values actually observed, and relatively simple objects used to aid observation, at least in the middle ranges of the dimension. Cultural contamination is avoided by calibration of the dimension on natural constants (phase shift temperatures of water, absence of molecular motion). As in the case of length, there are institutions which help to control semantic change. The Treaty of the Meter concerns itself with temperature as one of the seven fundamental dimensions of our universe. The various bureaus of standards are conducting basic research on temperature, and they also calibrate instruments for others.

Measurement: From Observation to Variable

This book is about achieving comparability in scientific empirical observation languages. Where dimensions in the physical sciences are concerned, the usual term would be *measurement*. I propose that measurement is a special case of observation, and that it requires the existence of variables. I further propose that, in science, as part of the development strategy for observation, there is constant pressure to create, and improve, variables.

There are a number of ideal attributes of dimensional analysis. The development of an observation language is towards these ideals. When fairly well along the developmental path, we can say that the dimension is represented in a mature variable, and measurement can be said to occur. A number of conditions are striven for in a mature observational technology:

1. The dimension is monothetic.

   A monothetic dimension is one where there is only one dimension captured by the variable. If two or more dimensions are conflated in the variable, and their relative presence varies from empirical case to empirical case, then comparability is compromised. Comparability is maximized by having a single dimension.

2. There is a standard, ideally a natural constant.

The monothetic dimension is represented in a standard. A natural constant for the standard maximizes comparability across empirical situations. Without a constant, the "meaning" of the variable will vary across different environments (often called systems). Having a natural constant as the foundation of the dimension strongly promotes comparability.

3. The dimension is named in unambiguous terms.

The dimension must be named unambiguously. If the dimension (or variable) has two or more names, or especially if the dimension shares a name with another dimension, then comparability is not assured.

4. The scale type of the variable is known.

Scale type is taken from the analysis of S. S. Stevens (1946). Every mature variable has a single scale type (nominal, ordinal, interval, ratio), and it is known. A major concern of Stevens in forming this typology of scales was to be clear about the permitted mathematical procedures in the subsequent analysis of the data. Our statistical techniques for investigating correlations (factor analysis, analysis of variance, regressions, etc.) all have logical requirements in terms of the properties of the scale types underlying the data to be analyzed. For the analysis to be comparable across cases and studies, the relationship between the scale type, and the quantitative procedures, must be an appropriate one. If it is not, then the comparability of the results is compromised. Consequently, the scale type is a factor in comparability.

5. The scale values have the property of uniqueness.

Scale value refers to the particular values that may be observed with a scale. If the dimension is length, the unit is the meter, foot, cubit, and so forth, and each observation will be represented by a symbol, in this case a natural number (say, 2 meters). Each symbol when used in this context must have the property of uniqueness.

Uniqueness is a property of natural numbers. Consequently, there is no ambiguity when numbers are the symbols for scale values. With natural numbers this property seems obvious and trivial, once it is pointed out. However, when the symbols being used are *not* numbers but words (such as granite, eye, protein, etc.), achieving uniqueness becomes much more problematic. A mature variable has achieved uniqueness in the scale values, and this helps to produce comparability.

6. The scale units are named in unambiguous terms.

Our American folk measuring system contains several terms for units that are ambiguous. Pint has at least two meanings (dry, wet), mile has at least two (statute, nautical), and ton has three (long, short, avoirdupois), all with different definitions. These different meanings refer to different values (e.g., a statute mile is 5,280 feet, a nautical mile is 6,080 feet). Comparability is compromised if the terms used to refer to units on a dimension are not named unambiguously. The names must have the property of uniqueness for comparability to be possible.

7. Training exists in how to observe the dimension.

There is no naive scientific observer. For observations to be comparable the same techniques and procedures must be used. The activity of observing must be comparable across instances. In a mature science the activity of observing is the subject of considerable training and detailed reporting. The more rigorous the training, the more likely that comparability of observations will result.

Training is a component of the mature variable. In the measurement of length it would seem that there is little training necessary because of the existence of devices called rulers. The story is somewhat more complex. It has always been the case that setting the national (or imperial) standard has been in the hands of a few specialists. No ordinary carpenter, making a cubit stick, would have had access to the pharaoh's forearm. And likewise today, the establishment of the standard for the meter is a job for highly trained specialists at the various national bureaus of standards. These specialists have been able to generate devices that reproduce the standard so that it is reasonably useful to the relevant people at an appropriate standard of accuracy. A carpenter (in the United States), for example, may want to measure to 1/16th of an inch, a cabinet maker to 1/64th. A metal worker or an auto mechanic may need to measure to 1/1000th of an inch.[17] We have meter sticks, but we also have micrometers. For many ranges of length there are cheap standardized devices that require some but not a great deal of training to use successfully. The existence of these relatively simple devices has greatly facilitated observational measurement by large numbers of people.

Other forms of observational measurement of length exist—say, the distance between galaxies, or between atoms—that use the meter as the unit but that no ordinary person has any capacity to perform. In this case one must have extensive special training and access to expensive and complicated devices, ones, furthermore, that do not give us a direct reading of the distance. Very large distances are measured with the Hubble "constant," and there is a good deal of discussion, even dispute, over the size of that constant. Most of us do not measure such distances ourselves but rely on specialists to do it for us. The same conditions apply in the case of temperature.

8. Social structure must be considered.

The entire aggregate of observers has to reach consensus on what procedures are to be used and what names are to be used if there is to be cross-group comparability of observational results. Mature sciences achieve this with conventions, regular meetings of participants to discuss definitions, procedures, and names.

9. Unambiguous names for objects must be used.

Every dimension must be observed at some point in space-time and must be manifest in some object to be observable. Far too little attention has been paid to the "object" problem, which will be examined in detail in the next chapter. The object being observed must be named unambiguously every time an observation takes place. Otherwise, no comparability can be assumed.

Notes

1. *Object* implies a tangible and discrete mass, and part of natural science makes observations of spaces (vacuums, deep space) and of matter that does not necessarily come in a discrete package (such as sandstone, iron, or weather). Nevertheless, every dimension has to be manifest somewhere and sometime, and it is a dimension manifest in something else. I will use *object* to refer to that something else where the dimension is manifest.

2. Our word *length* is ambiguous in the natural language of American English. It refers to an abstract dimension (of extension). Dimension and length are also used to refer to the length, width, and height of some object—say, a building, or a box. Length, width, and height are all measured by the same dimension, length (as opposed to mass, say). When I use *length* I mean the abstract notion of extension, not the sense of dimension and length which contrasts width, height, and length.

3. The distribution and nature of such natural culture measuring systems in present-day nonliterate cultures is unknown. We have only bits and pieces of a few of them. Given the rapid disappearance of such cultures in the twentieth century, it may be too late to recover any large number of them. But some of them should be recoverable, and it would be productive to do so.

4. There has been exchange between locales of worked objects (copper, obsidian) for many millennia. How the various locales understood dimensions such as length and mass under these circumstances (before the advent of multilocale polities) is an

interesting problem. The problem of how value is created, and assigned to objects, is at issue here. The piece is one starting point, but pieces vary in dimensions, including length, area, volume, mass, and quality. Surely it did not take long before these dimensions were imagined. Once imagined, some shared understanding of them is a likely product of exchange.

5. Perhaps the merchants kept track of all these variations and were able to calculate the relationship that each had to the other. There is another alternative, which is that the merchant carried his own measuring devices, and bought or sold according to his own estimate of the amount of cloth, wine, oil, and so forth, in the transaction. A clear picture of how this problem was solved by merchants operating in Europe would be most welcome.

6. The peace of the market is an apparently universal property of marketplaces. Someone is responsible for the marketplace, for solving disputes that arise in the marketplace, and it is their responsibility to try to maintain peace. For a view of how this worked in a "peripheral" market in Africa, see Bohannan and Bohannan (1968:146-193).

7. There is a conflation of three different concepts in the English term *ruler*. It refers to the legitimate holder of a position of authority, to the device used to measure length, and implies a set of legitimate procedures to govern. Linguistically these three conditions seem not to be connected in other agrarian states. But the conditions are often associated with one another in those same states. An investigation of this association ought to be productive.

8. Almost all the historical analysis of weights and measures pays attention to the translation of the natural culture units into modern units, and in the ratios of the various units (Powell 1989, 1990; Dilke 1987). There is virtually no attention paid to the social structure, and the use, of these weights and measures. An effort to elucidate the social history of these efforts to control variation should pay handsome rewards.

9. SI refers to the Système International d'Unités (International System of Units). A successor to the metric system, this is governed by the International Committee of Weights and Measures, with headquarters in France.

10. Many European natural cultures used a principle of doubling/halving in their measurement languages (cup, pint, quart is an example). This shift to base 10 was a radical change, and one that Adams objected to in 1821. Duration in musical notation also uses the dividing-by-two principle (whole notes, half notes, quarter notes, etc.).

11. A major innovation was to express volume in terms of length, and then to link mass with length by making a specific volume of water the standard for mass. By this stroke all the different systems of measurement of length, and mass, were reduced to one. For science this was a major step, for it encouraged the understanding of the relationships of dimensions, which when combined with base 10 were important in the search for fundamental laws.

12. The U.S. measuring system (containing such units as inch, ounce, second, and degree but two pints, two miles [statute, nautical], and several pounds [troy, avoirdupois, etc.]) was cut loose from the customary definitions in 1893 and has been defined in terms of metric units ever since (Chisholm 2002:696).

13. We are dealing here with a problem in social control. A number of disciplines have established institutions which virtually freeze, and bring under rational control, one of the most powerful forces in human cultures, semantic drift. How the consensual agreements achieve authority, and power, need explication. Presumably the editors of scientific publications are very important participants in this process. A study of the evolution and operation of such consensual control measures would be very useful.

14. Ratio scales have a true zero. Presumably, for an object to manifest a dimension (e.g., length), the value on that dimension cannot be zero. If it is zero, then the dimension is not manifest. A point in Euclidian geometry, for example, has no dimension of length. By definition it has only position. Can one say that the point has zero length? Or must one say that the point does not manifest the dimension of length? If the latter is the case, then the zero exists for mathematical purposes and serves no observation purpose.

15. There is another aspect of cumulation of knowledge that is linked with progress in observation. When a new skill or technique becomes available there is often a vast increase in observations, and subsequently a comparable increase in systemic knowledge. The various forms of the microscope and the telescope are striking evidence of this, but the same holds true for the thermometer and for many others. There is every reason, therefore, to spend considerable effort on observation. And I will argue below that exactly the same conditions hold in what is called social science. Here also the observation technologies generate, and constrain, knowledge. Advances in observation often result in major increases in knowledge.

16. Phase shift refers to the change when water is cooled from 1°C to –1°C, and from 101°C to 99°C. It changes from liquid to solid, or from a gas to a liquid. Most matter is subject to phase shifts, at appropriate temperatures and pressures. The change in temperature does not explain the phase shift, for a change from 53°C to 51°C does not result in the same shift from liquid to solid of water (at one atmosphere of pressure.) Phase shifts are often called qualitative changes.

17. The differences in these figures are striking. The official standards for the inch are metric in the United States, and have been since 1893. The 1/16th and 1/64th divisions of the inch are based on the old European doubling principle (1/2 of 1 = 1/2, 1/2 of 1/2 = 1/4, 1/2 of 1/4=1/8, 1/2 of 1/8 = 1/16, and so on). The machinists' practice demands much smaller units, and so they are using a decimal division, but of the inch!

CHAPTER FOUR

~

The Problem of Objects

To achieve a replicable observation of the dimension of temperature, length, or mass, we must be extremely specific and clear about where we go to observe that dimension. The observer must be able to specify the location of that observation in such a way that all subsequent scientists who wish to observe it will know exactly where to do it. Therefore, the clear and unambiguous identification of the object is crucial for scientific dimensional observation.

An example from biology is instructive. Early on in the study of malaria it was suspected that mosquitoes were part of the picture. To test this idea some investigations used any handy mosquito and (not surprisingly) came up empty. As a consequence of the negative results, the mosquito part of the effort was largely abandoned for a while. It was not until only the anopheline mosquitoes were put under the microscope that progress in understanding the vector could be made. Mosquitoes in general caused vast uncertainty in the search. Much more precision about one of the objects (the insect vector) was needed (Desowitz 1991).

The object problem has apparently been solved in much of physical science, and relatively little formal attention is now paid to it. Many objects are no longer seen as problematic, or as worthy of discussion and research. The periodic table of elements is used but not investigated. Once established, the objects are taken for granted, as the SI system of dimensions is by the vast majority of those who use it.

Taxonomies

We as a species perceive a very large number of objects, and so does every natural culture. That number is too large for anyone to remember, and we have divided those objects into kinds of objects, in many instances several times. Science has a large number of scientific lists of kinds of objects: elementary particles, chemical elements, rock (igneous, sedimentary), soil particles (sand, silt, clay), celestial objects, and animals and plants. Every such list is a typology. One of the most important features of a scientific typology is that the categories are exhaustive and mutually exclusive. They are classical categories in Lakoff's terms (1987).

All these scientific classifications of objects operate with the principle that every object that is included is a single kind of thing. An eagle soaring in the sky would not be included in a classification of a celestial object. Leopards would not be included in a classification of plants. For this to be the case, there must be a definition of the set of objects, and all potential objects must be either inside or outside the set. The problem here is to construct categories for "kinds of things" which are comparable. There must be clear criteria by which objects are assigned to membership. For the periodic table, the kinds of things are chemical elements. Water, earth, air, and fire are no longer candidates for the domain.

Within the classification, uniqueness holds for each of the classes or types. The classes must be exhaustive and mutually exclusive. Furthermore, the names for each object and for each type of object must be clear and unambiguous. Most such names (e.g., planet, galaxy, oxygen, plant) are words, not numbers, and so the forces of semantic drift will be powerful and must be controlled. These typologies constitute the list of objects where science goes to observe dimensions.

There has been relatively little discussion of scientific typologies of objects, at least that has surfaced in the general scientific literature. The major exception is biological systematics, where there are vigorous controversies. The purposes for which such typologies were constructed in the first place, and their uses today, are often not obvious to the general reader.

In the case of living organisms, the identity of the object (at least at the organism level) for science is now specified in the Linnaean taxonomy. It has been clear for a long time that the individual live organisms we perceive can be grouped into a much smaller number of categories of living kinds. A "living kind" is a class of organism. Within the circumscribed territory of a natural culture with a small territory, the least-general level of living kind corresponds to the scientific category of genus. The living kinds available in southern Arizona in the 1990s will not be the same collection as the living kinds available in southern Arizona in the 1490s. Living kinds are not species, for the species concept now has important implications of distribution in secular time and very large areas. (See Atran [1990] and Berlin [1992] for important discussions of these matters.) Lions and sheep and barley and palm trees, as categories of kinds of animals and plants, are clearly named in the earliest writing from Mesopotamia and Egypt. Every natural culture so far investigated has at least one of these typologies (Brown 1991; Berlin 1992).

At the beginning of modern European exploration of the non-European world many unfamiliar animals and plants were encountered. There was as yet no scientific observation language. Europeans adapted some of the local names (e.g., tomato, avocado, tobacco, cocoa, coca, maize, tea, coffee) and transferred some of their own names (e.g., turkey, corn). The descriptions of these living kinds were written in the European languages, either the scholarly language, Latin, or in the natural languages (Portuguese, Spanish, French, etc.). And it turned out that it was extremely difficult to translate effectively from, say, Spanish to English, so that the reader could be sure that the living kind described in Spanish was the same as, or different from, the living kind described in English. The several natural languages of Europe were not up to the job of unambiguously describing and cataloging the various living kinds that were encountered.

Two of the earliest solutions to this dilemma were to bring specimens home, preferably live ones (including humans), and to bring home detailed, color, two-dimensional representations of the specimens. Today the nonscientist tends to regard the transport of living humans as a terrible injustice and to regard the "paintings" and "drawings" as art work rather than as crucial illustrations of living kinds (as in the bird "paintings" by James Audubon). Their original function was to represent the observed details of exotic living kinds visually (as well as in words).

Our current solution to the language problem was established in the eighteenth century by a Swede, Karl Linne (he called himself Carolus Linnaeus in Latin), who not only classified a prodigious number of living kinds personally but also established a classification format for those life forms. The binomial form referred to two levels of classification. The central plane of the classification was a kind of thing, the genus. Species were subtypes of the genus, and there were subtypes of the species (races, varieties). Every genus was a kind of thing, containing species. And every species was a kind of a thing, containing individual organisms.

When this system became dominant it was assumed that species were fixed entities, and the purpose was to organize the vast number of living

kinds into a much smaller number of categories so that they might be cata-
logued, remembered more easily, and discussed. It was not until the mid-
nineteenth century with Darwin and Wallace that it was firmly established
both that species were not fixed and that all these different forms were related by shared descent. It may well be the case that shared descent is first
identified with respect to language (Hoenigswald and Wiener 1987). And it
was later still before our understanding of genetics as the mechanism of inheritance began to take hold. Yet despite these massive changes in understanding and purpose, the binomial classification system is still used to map
the world of organisms and is still evolving.

Today one major purpose of this classification scheme is to represent
shared descent, and therefore evolution. But there is a prior and continuing
purpose, the accurate and unambiguous description and naming of the many
different living kinds to be found.[1]

The observation and subsequent description of each organism involves
analytically segmenting each organism into traits or characters, and many of
these are organized as dimensions (e.g., size, limbs, organs, form, color).

Some of the general principles of dimensional analysis apply to typologies
as well. Kinds of objects must be established, and the categories should be exhaustive and mutually exclusive. The names applied should be unambiguous.
Anyone with the requisite training in use of the key can identify already
known forms and describe new forms in ways that would communicate with
vastly reduced ambiguity (when compared with any natural language).

The observation languages for both dimensions and whole organisms are
composed of technical terms which are words. But these words are not func-
tioning in a natural language. They have instead been made part of a technical language, and this is done to strip them of their multiple meanings. The
drive has been to reduce ambiguity to as close to zero as possible.

For example, the word *fruit* occurs in natural American English and in a
technical lexicon in botany. In natural American English, a fruit is fleshy,
sweet, vegetable (rather than animal) and includes strawberries, bananas,
peaches, apples, and oranges. In botany, the fruit is the matured ovary of the
pistil of a flower and includes apples, bananas, and strawberries but also eggplant, tomato, squash, and olives. Some living kinds occur in both lists, but
some do not. The botanical definition and use of the word is virtually without
ambiguity. The American folk term is ambiguous. The two observation languages use some of the same terms but with significantly different meanings.

The terms for relationships between variables in taxonomy and paleon-
tology use words, not numbers. Descent, homology, and analogy are judg-

ments of the relationships between variables (and species) over time and to changes in their environment.[2] The essential requirement in the use of these words is uniqueness.

The organism, one object to be studied, is analytically segmented into parts, and the characteristics of those parts are studied. In length and temperature we are operating with a concept of a dimension manifest in many objects and processes. That dimension is defined independently of the object itself.

In taxonomy the dimensions of objects are variable in distribution. We have found universally occurring aspects of organisms, such as cells, volume, mass, temperature, and an external membrane. We have also found less generally occurring aspects of organisms, such as limbs, vertebral columns, seeds, and roots. When we analytically approach the organism from the point of view of these dimensions we are not interested in the whole of that organism. Rather we are observing specified aspects or dimensions of that thing.

If this analysis is accepted, then clearly we have a circle of mutual dependence and relevance of the dimensions, and the classification of the object. Each needs the other, although the major purpose of one is a minor purpose of the other. A major purpose of every classification/taxonomy is to organize numbers of whole objects. Good dimensions are only one of the means. A major purpose of dimensional analysis is to find relationships between the dimensions. Specifying the object is a necessary means to that end but is not the end itself.

All typologies are constructed for a purpose. Adams and Adams in their useful book on classification in archaeology make the point that the purpose of any classification must be clearly stated, and it must be kept in mind as the classification is constructed, used, and changed (1991). The utility of a classification is to a large degree a function of the purpose for which it was constructed. If it is to be used for a different purpose than the original one, then the structure of that classification must be rethought and perhaps changed.

There is a distinction between the purpose(s) of the typology and the purpose(s) of the scientist. The typology must serve at least one purpose of the scientist, but the scientist can, and often does, have other purposes as well. There are several scientific interests in the object. One is to identify the object so that dimensional analysis may proceed. Another is to understand and explain as much as possible about the objects themselves, for there are scientists interested in knowing as much as possible about a class of objects. Natural history, material science, and ecology come to mind. Another purpose is to understand and explain development in nature (evolution is one form of development).

All of these purposes demand an accurate and unambiguous identification of the kinds of objects within the domain. If a typology (the periodic table, for example) reveals the structure of nature, classifies objects in parsimonious ways, and also reveals development, then we have a very powerful typology of objects. But no typology need serve all these purposes. As Adams and Adams have argued, the typology is designed to do a specific task (1991). A particular typology may or may not be appropriate and adequate for other scientific tasks, and the evaluation of the typology must keep the tasks clearly separated.

An important question is how to achieve that state of uniqueness usually associated with numbers when our lexicon is words. With numbers, uniqueness is true by definition. With words, which often come from natural language in the first place, ambiguity and semantic drift are camels always trying to get their noses under the tent flaps.[3] Eliminating ambiguity in the observational language is extremely important and extremely hard to achieve.

Some of the procedures for eliminating ambiguity and cultural contamination in dimensions are appropriate for object description. To briefly review them, a mature variable is monothetic, is calibrated with a natural constant, has an unambiguous name, has a known scale type, has scale values which have the property of uniqueness, has scale units with unambiguous names, names the objects, involves training, and has a social structure that constrains semantics.

Some of these apply in the case of object descriptions. Typologies of objects are like nominal scales, in that the categories should have the property of uniqueness (mutually exclusive, exhaustive). This implies that the domain or universe of the typology is quite well specified. A monothetic category is the goal. A monothetic feature would mean that there is a single necessary and sufficient attribute that serves to place an object in a category. Prototype theory would seem to imply that a monothetic criterion is unnecessary, and perhaps in some cases impossible. But any scientific typology needs to have types that have uniqueness (Adams and Adams 1991).

The natural constant is present in biological systematics, for there is stress on having type specimens for reference and training. Certainly an unambiguous name is needed for each type of object. Scale type is irrelevant for a classification, as are scale values and scale unit names. We are naming the object, so naming the object is irrelevant, although the domain may not be irrelevant.

Training and social structure to control the semantics are in place in systematics and apparently not needed for the periodic table or the map of ob-

jects in the sky. The largest and most contentious object classification language is biological systematics, and in this case both extensive training and
a social structure to control the meaning of the terms are in place. The training of practitioners is part of the solution, and it occurs in every discipline.
Every individual is thoroughly immersed in at least one natural culture, and
so is equipped with a large amount of working perceptual and interpretive
software. A new set of perceptual responses must be installed, and this starts
during training. Part of this will occur during formal lessons, as in classrooms
and reading assignments. But another part, at least in the group-work sciences, occurs as part of socialization into the profession, in work on-site (in
the laboratory, at the observatory, on the field trip, etc.).

One of the jobs of this socialization period is to create, maintain, and fine
tune the ability to operate within the scientific culture. And a major part of
this effort is to train the initiates in operating an observational language
without ambiguity and one that is totally shared with fellow workers. Of
course the degree of uncertainty which is achieved varies from discipline to
discipline.[4]

The use of simple devices as measuring instruments is often not possible.
The dimensions of the organisms, and of organs, can be measured with rulers
in some cases. Standard body temperature can be taken with a thermometer.
But in making the decision as to whether some part of an organism is or is
not like an already specified kind, a device will not avail. The issue here is
determining the standard with which one compares the form to be observed.
The major way to reduce uncertainty is to have an example of the standard
for comparison.

This central role of the type specimen accounts for the practice of bringing back the exotic forms, of detailed realistic drawings of those forms, of
standard collections, and of museums to house the drawings and the specimens. The largely unambiguous observation language of taxonomy is dependent upon standards, and these are ideally collections of the organisms (specimens) or detailed drawings of specimens, ideally done in the natural setting.
Part of the training of a taxonomist involves becoming familiar with collections of specimens.

Semantic drift is now controlled with frequent conferences on nomenclature. The most effective way to get an aggregate of diverse people from different natural cultures to stabilize the uses of terms is to convince them that
such a goal is necessary, gather them together to discuss how a given term is
to be used, get them to agree on single meanings for terms, and then to en-
courage if not enforce such uses in the future. Such conferences take place
regularly in systematics.[5]

There is a hierarchy of organizations which deal with the meanings of words in biology. At the top is the International Union of Biological Sciences (IUBS) (the 28th Congress of the IUBS was held in Cairo in 2004). The International Congress of Systematic and Evolutionary Biology (IC-SEB) is a later creation (its sixth congress was held in Patras, Greece, in 2002).[6] It in turn sponsors an International Commission on Zoological Nomenclature. The fourth edition of the International Code of Zoological Nomenclature was adopted by the IUBS and published in 1999. The commission is the authority that decides on zoological nomenclature, but its charter of authority is the IUBS.

The next question to deal with is how the comparative observation languages deal with contamination from some natural culture. How is an observation language calibrated across time and space? First, there is now an observation language for the characteristics of each organism. Largely but not necessarily conducted in English at the moment, the basic parts of life forms have achieved stability in the observation language. We now apparently know enough about anatomy and genomes so that there are few if any surprises.

Furthermore, the lexicon for describing each individual part is also quite stable. This system is based on naturally occurring forms, such as limbs, cell nuclei, nerve cells, flowers, and leaves. A rice plant will have stems, roots, leaves, seeds, and so forth whether it occurs in China, India, or Senegal. And a lion has forelimbs, hind limbs, a tail, and a social system whether it is in Africa, China, or Assyria. The underlying structure of the dimensions will be the same kind of thing, no matter where it is found. It is stable, and it does not vary because it is found in Mongolia or the Kalahari. It is therefore a matter of choosing the right lexicon to describe the manifestations of this underlying structure. It is very likely that the structure of nature is constraining the choices made in observational categories.

I have presented a view of a biological taxonomy which is now stable and successful, and yet we are all aware of strong disagreements and serious problems within taxonomy. Those disputes, I claim, are not in the realm of the empirical observation language but instead involve other issues. Two of the major issues are the assignment of individual organisms to taxa and the nature of a species.

Once the organism has been described, it is assigned to a genus and species in a classification scheme. Assignment of the organism to a local living kind is usually not problematic. But the organization of higher levels of the taxonomy can be very difficult and problematic. Every such assignment now carries evolutionary and structure of nature implications, for these are the purposes of the scientists involved.

The problem of species is more complex. There seems to be agreement that local living kinds exist. But our analysis of species has now extended to the whole globe and to the entire history of life. The nature of a species over secular time and huge amounts of space is very different from the similarities of living kinds in a small area over a handful of generations. The species problem is whether we can reasonably talk of species over these large spans of space and time (see Hull 1992). One of the problems is that the taxonomy was originally designed for a synchronic purpose and with the assumption of the fixity of species. The fixed species assumption has now been abandoned, and a new purpose is now dominant (mapping shared descent). If we were starting from scratch today, would we design our typology this way? Some of the problems with the taxonomy may be caused by nature. But it is a good bet, at least to this outsider, that some of them are caused by trying to use the typology to achieve a purpose that was far from the minds of the designers. There is a movement to adopt a new system of description and nomenclature, PhyloCode (Pennisi 2001).

Note, however, that the synchronic purpose of classification is still operative, still effective, and, if anything, more crucial for human welfare than when the taxonomy was designed. I refer of course to public health, where the valid identification of such elements as bacteria, viruses, nematodes, and deer mice is crucial to understanding and combating outbreaks of disease.

In taxonomy generally there is frequent disagreement over the relationship of individual forms. And there is disagreement over which characteristics should be privileged in that assignment. But there is little disagreement over what the fundamental analytic segments are and how they should be described. These disputes do not challenge the effectiveness of the empirical observation language.

The empirical observation language does, of course, improve. As science has progressed we have understood more and more about the anatomy of life forms. We have discovered many new life forms, we have added new dimensions to our lists (e.g., DNA), and new technology has permitted a larger variety of descriptions to be made. In consequence, the descriptive framework has developed and will continue to develop. Quite possibly it will never be finished. The effort to root out cultural contamination and ambiguity and to increase precision, accuracy, and validity has been very successful, and it continues.

Social Objects and Folk Taxonomies

There are many objects of scientific interest other than organisms. Some of these are stable and known (chemical elements, for instance), and some are still undergoing discovery (e.g., elementary particles). Some of the objects of scientific interest include organisms but are not a single organism: groups (prides, pods), populations, food webs, communities.

Organisms do not live by themselves—many reproduce sexually, and there are often social units of organisms (terms of venery recognize this) and populations. Furthermore, members of the same type do not live in isolation from other types of organisms—there are food sources, predators, parasites, symbionts, and decomposers by the score. So there are "communities" of different kinds of organisms. These social entities (groups, populations, and communities) are perhaps as real, and certainly as important for our understanding, as the organism itself. When the objects are aggregates or groups of organisms the perception and classification of the object are often problematic.

Our ability to conceptualize, describe, and classify these relational and social "objects" is far less developed than is our taxonomy of organisms. Two great advantages of the organism in this process include that it is firmly bounded (by a membrane) and it is related to other organisms by descent. Descent produces a great deal of similarity among exemplars of the same living kind.

Boundaries are central in our thinking about objects. But it is a rare social set that has a boundary as clear and functional as the external membrane of an organism or cell. The lack of a clear boundary has posed a very difficult problem for the scientist when trying to specify the social object. Taxonomies and other forms of classification cannot be formulated until we are clear about the objects that are being classified. When we deal with these social sets it is not clear what the objects are when we cannot find firm boundaries.

An effective scientific typology is one whose categories or types have uniqueness (exhaustive, mutually exclusive). This property demands that we draw boundaries around the type. The similarity that is the product of shared descent helps us draw those boundaries, as does the external membrane that defines the organism.

I suggest that our scientific efforts to create typologies of objects are profoundly affected by both the ubiquitous folk biological taxonomies and the scientist's general knowledge of organism taxonomy.

All human cultures apparently contain taxonomies of living kinds, and so the activity is clearly deeply ingrained (Brown 1991). All scientific classifications must utilize the uniqueness principle, which entails that each class is exhaustive and mutually exclusive. As Adams and Adams point out, these features are essential for science. As they and others have noted, a taxonomy is a special kind of classification. Taxonomies are hierarchical, whereas plain classifications are not. Folk taxonomies are also hierarchical. We therefore have, from our natural culture, a template of organizing living kinds (and by metaphorical extension other kinds of "objects") in hierarchical classifications. All folk taxonomies (of life forms) recognize descent as a principle and account for similarities of at least some living kinds (parents and children) by descent. This observation is by and large correct.

The current biological taxonomy (of organisms) has two major purposes: it is a catalog of life forms and it purports to represent shared descent in the evolutionary sense. Most human cultures name the objects in their universe, create taxonomies for some of those objects, and create a story that accounts for the way things came to be the way they are (usually called origin myths). When we try to classify other kinds of objects I suggest that we use classifications that are analogs of taxonomies of living kinds.

It is very difficult for the educated person to conceive of a taxonomy that does not have both purposes. Even the periodic table of elements has the two purposes. When we try to conceive and classify objects we are strongly inclined to build a taxonomy and to include an evolutionary principle. We are bathed by a kind of semantic universal of biological taxonomizing, as it were, and it is extremely difficult to think one's way outside it.

If this analysis is accepted, then it is clear why there are severe problems with our attempts to establish social kinds of objects. Boundaries are a problem for observation and classification. Social objects are frequently open systems. This poses a challenge for establishing observational units and for classification. Furthermore, the background radiation from taxonomy encourages us to think in hierarchical and descent terms, which may or may not be appropriate.

Establishing comparability in the objects is then a serious problem for the social objects. But not having established mature criteria does not mean that quest for knowledge has to be abandoned. The problem might exist because no comparability can ever be established. Alternatively, the problem may exist because we have not yet tried to solve it with an effective strategy.

Social Objects and Causation

O'Meara, Sperber, and others have presented arguments that causal entities must be physical entities (O'Meara 1997, 1999, 2001; Sperber 1996). Because culture, society, and institutions, for example, are superorganic and not physical entities they cannot be causal agents. The individual organism and its physical properties are the only physical parts of the human behavior system and thus the only ones with causal power. If this position on causality becomes normal science, then culture and society may turn out to be metaphors like caloric and phlogiston. During one phase of the evolution of a science they were attractive in that they were the most parsimonious solutions to problems. Later, as observation and theory had improved, they turn out to be unnecessary, and were discarded, to become curiosities of history. It is conceivable that culture and society will have the same fate.

And yet one is moved to raise a problem. Any science of human behavior will have to deal with the evident fact that human behavior is highly variable, and that particular forms of learned human behavior are shared by some individuals but not by a substantial number of others. Many have argued that these conjunctions of learned behaviors (culture1) display system-like properties. One eagerly awaits learning how this new ontology, with its content-specific modules supposedly found in all members of the whole species, accounts for the spatially and temporally structured variation of behavior that I have called culture1. Either a way will have to be found to accommodate and reformulate the information of culture1, or the concept of culture1 will have to be kept. And if it is kept we will have to rethink causation.

For the moment it seems premature to dispense with the concept of culture1. It is a summary of important features of humans (and, to a small extent, of chimpanzees).

I have argued that comparability is necessary for science (and for many other human activities) and that comparability requires unique names. It is worth recapitulating at this point how the problems we isolated in chapter 2 have been solved in the realm of dimensions (length and temperature are the examples) and objects. Two problems were identified: cultural contamination and ambiguity in the language.

There is a challenge to finding the same kinds of thing, which may be labeled the problem of cultural contamination. In the case of a dimension, establishing that it is a kind of a thing involves splitting until the dimension is monothetic. (A polythetic concept always involves two or more kinds of thing, combined in unknown proportions.) Finding a natural constant is a great aid to universality. Applications are more valid if there is some sort of object which can be used to manifest the standard.

The dimension of length is now defined as a property of light moving in space and time. Temperature is defined as a property of matter, and the standard includes the two phase shift changes of water. In each case there are natural constants, and in each case the dimension can confidently be thought to be monothetic. For objects the problems are similar. We attempt to establish kinds of objects and classifications of kinds of objects. In every case there seems to be a set of dimensions observed, and one or more values on one or more dimensions are used as the criteria for deciding that two objects are or are not of the same kind. We attempt to be as specific as possible and to construct concepts that are exhaustive and mutually exclusive. Among the more problematic kinds of objects are life forms and social "objects" like communities and populations.

There is the companion problem of establishing unambiguous language. Different natural languages sometimes have different names for the same thing and usually different names for different things. Natural languages easily accommodate ambiguity in naming things. Furthermore, natural languages are subject to semantic drift. Establishing monothetic dimensions with natural constants is part of the battle against ambiguity, for the kind of thing is held constant. But there is still a problem with the language.

The solution to the problem of ambiguity in names is to find names with the property of uniqueness. Natural numbers inherently have that property, and that is one of the reasons that science tries to be quantitative. But there are many words in science that are not numbers (such as *meter* and *Canis canis*). How those words become and remain semantically unique is a crucial part of the story. The solution is a social structure that agrees to the value of uniqueness, is able to agree on a single meaning for each word, and is able to confine the scientific community's use of that word to the unique meaning.

This principle applies to both dimensions and objects. The conference associated with SI has authority over the fundamental dimensions. There are other conferences that have similar authority in other domains (e.g., biological systematics, phonology).

It is important to note that in every case we have a developmental process. It is never the case that a dimension is conceived from whole cloth (although some objects—quasars and muons, for example—may be) and forever afterwards is stable. All of our dimensions have begun, often in some natural culture, and have developed in unpredictable but subsequently understandable ways. The same is true of most objects. Much effort has been, is, and will be invested in basic and applied research on the dimensions and objects. New ones would be welcome. Discovering problems with old solutions is welcome. Solving those problems is also welcome. Precision, validity, and reliability in the observations are crucial and precious to science. The search for these elements is institutionalized, and the result is development in secular time.

Natural language despotism was included in the argument of chapter 2. The position taken by some is that there is only natural culture and natural language. The only concepts that exist are in natural culture. I contend that the facts presented in chapters 3 and 4 constitute a powerful argument for the existence of scientific concepts, scientific culture, and scientific language.

The search for monothetic and universal dimensions and objects is not char-acteristic, as a whole, of any natural culture. The control over meaning, and over semantic drift, as a whole, is not characteristic of any natural culture.

Science is socially constructed, but it does not construct in the same way that natural cultures do. Science is quite different. Science is not Western ethnoscience.

Notes

1. This function is necessary for any dimensional study within and between the relevant organisms. The successful investigation of Lyme disease, for example, re-quired the accurate taxonomic identification of the disease organism itself, of the an-imal vectors, and of the animal reservoirs. Without these identifications and de-scriptions, no progress would have been possible in unraveling the disease or in finding a general treatment.

2. Numerical classification (cf. Sneath and Sokal 1973), so vigorous over the past few decades, has tried to substitute mathematical analysis for word analysis. Some of the underlying dimensions are also being converted to ordinal or higher scale types. There is a movement, then, for systematics to move towards more quantitative scale types in observation and to use formal mathematics in the analysis of the relation-ships of the dimensions.

3. This phrase is commonly found but rarely explained. Imagine a desert in the winter, with the temperature down around 0°C. Imagine a smallish tent, with a small fire, and a number of people huddling around to keep warm. Imagine also a largish camel, outside in the cold, wanting to be warm. The camel puts its nose under the flap of the tent, seeking warmth. Imagine that the camel, finding warmth inside the tent, joins the others already there. Now imagine a warmish tent containing a fire, a number of people, and a camel or two. An equivalent phrase in English is: Give them an inch and they take a mile.

4. That there is uncertainty need not distress us. Uncertainty is everywhere, and it can not be reduced to zero. We must always acknowledge it, take it into account, work around it, and attempt to reduce it. A major part of our effort in science must be to understand it, to analyze as exactly as we can how that uncertainty affects our conclusions, and to reduce that uncertainty by theoretical, technological, and social means.

5. Comparative biology could not function with words in the measurement lexi-con if those words did not have the quality of uniqueness. It must be there. The only question is how it is created and enforced.

6. There are also codes for bacteria and for plants, whose principles differ in some ways from the zoological practice (Ride 1999:xxiii).

PART III

COMPARABILITY IN CULTURAL ANTHROPOLOGY: DIMENSIONS AND OBJECTS

Part III examines several investigation traditions in cultural anthropology, looking into the quality and degree of development of the empirical observation languages. The reader is reminded that culture1 is the meaning intended here.

The question being asked is whether comparability has been achieved, and if so how. I will argue, and hopefully demonstrate, that some of these systems are quite mature and cross-culturally valid as empirical observation languages for culture1. Each tells us many things that we would like to know, and each deals with at least some of the challenges to comparability. Some are more developed than others, and that is to be expected. All demonstrate the relevance of the observation language principles extracted in part II and respond to the challenges summarized in part I.

I argue that successful empirical observation languages are being developed. I conclude that we have made substantial progress in creating a necessary condition for social science, scientific empirical observation languages.

CHAPTER FIVE

~

Phonology/Phonetics

All human societies have and use at least one natural language.[1] These natural languages are large, complex, and a major form of communication and information storage for the humans who speak them. All natural languages are learned by humans as part of social experience and are therefore a part of culture1. Natural language is an appropriate subject for analysis by dimensions and objects and for developing a scientific empirical observation language. As the reader will see, the phonological system analysis is perhaps the most developed of our scientific empirical observation languages for culture.

No two natural languages are identical. Phonology, morphology, syntax rules, and semantics all differ from slightly to massively between languages. These differences are responsible for the difficulty one has in speaking a "foreign" tongue without an accent, for the difficulties with translation from one language to another, and more profoundly for the difficulties in communication between the bearers of two different natural languages and cultures. These differences pose problems for communication, obviously. As we have seen in chapter 2, they also pose problems for scientific analysis and for the very existence of scientific analysis.

Very few native speakers of a natural language are aware of the vast complexity and structural order in the language they speak. Finding the variation and studying it have been major efforts of research and of consciousness.

When Europeans (and presumably others, such as speakers of Arabic and Chinese) made contact with native speakers of very different unwritten natural languages, it was hard to hear what the others were saying, and almost impossible to understand it. With more exposure, some were able to learn to speak and understand the target language.[2]

There was, however, the problem of how to represent the target language in writing. Early on, the Western Europeans used their own Roman-derived alphabet to represent the sounds of the target language and used grammatical concepts from some European tradition for analysis. Neither of these strategies worked very well. Distinctions made by Europeans were not necessarily present in the target language, and distinctions made in the target language were not necessarily present in the European language. Some native-language distinctions were projected onto the target languages, and many distinctions were missed altogether.

In Western European linguistics the effort of dealing with "exotic" languages of small-scale societies and exotic civilizations has been with us since at least the conquest of Mexico. Spaniards tried to represent Nahuatl and other Mesoamerican languages in the symbols of the Roman alphabet. Later the Jesuits who worked in northern North America represented Iroquois and other languages with Roman script, and also with Latin grammatical categories. These were rather crude approximations to the local reality, and over time the crudity of the approximation came to be recognized. A way to represent the sound systems of each language in a common observation language was needed.

Over the last several centuries there has arisen a scholarly tradition in Western Europe whose goal is the scientific study of the structure of any natural language. There has been development of the descriptive languages for several subsystems of language and development of theory of the phenomena. The subsystems include (but are not limited to) phonetics (sound production), phonology (the meaningful sound system of a natural language), morphology (meaningful units), syntax (rules for combining morphemes) and semantics. For the rest of this chapter I will concentrate on the sound part of the story.

One of the first problems to be solved was how to hear, and represent, the multitude of sounds being produced in these various natural languages. The study of the great variety of the sounds eventually emerged as the discipline of phonetics. What was being heard and how it could be represented were both solved by early in the twentieth century. An International Phonetic Association was formed, training courses were established in London, and standards were promulgated. Students learned how to hear the sounds in the course of their training and continued by practicing their skills professionally.

The problem of representation was solved by the invention of a special writing system, now called the International Phonetic Alphabet, or IPA (International Phonetic Association, 1999). In the first third of the twentieth century there were two important theoretical discoveries: the phoneme and the sound feature.

Every speaker of a human language produces a vast number of different sounds. Only some of them are relevant for the morphemic, syntactic, and semantic systems. A classic example is the phenomenon of aspirated stops in American English.[3]

In American English there are a series of unvoiced stops /p, t, k/. When we say out loud the following pairs of words—pain, Spain; top, stop; kin, skin—and we listen carefully, we can hear (and feel) that the words beginning with /s/ are different from the words beginning with /p, t, k/. One difference is that the initial stops (words starting with /p, t, k/) are followed by breathiness (aspiration), whereas the words starting with /s/ are not. We can represent them in the following way: [pʰin] versus [spin]; [tʰop] versus [stop]; [kʰin] versus [skin]. In some contexts the voiceless stop /p, t, k/ is followed by breathiness, or aspiration [pʰ, tʰ, kʰ], and in others it is not. A general rule can be written: Initial voiceless stops are aspirated, others are not.

If as an experiment one tries to pronounce spin as [spʰin] or pin as [pin], the native speaker will say that you sound funny or strange, but they will not think that [pin] means something different from [pʰin]. The contrast between aspiration and nonaspiration of a voiceless stop does not correlate with a difference in semantic meaning. The contrast is not phonemic (Lass 1984:15–18).

If one now listens to the Indo-European languages of India, one can also hear aspirated stops. But here one finds that the presence or absence of aspiration after a stop *is* correlated with a difference in meaning. In Bengali, for example, /ga/ (skin) and /gʰa/ (wound) are different only in the aspiration, as are /cap/ (pressure) and /cʰap/ (print).[4] In Hindi /pal/ ("moment") contrasts with /pʰal/ ("fruit"), and /kal/ ("time") with /kʰal/ (hide, skin).[5] The contrast between aspiration and nonaspiration of an initial stop does correlate with a difference in semantic meaning. The contrast is phonemic (see Lass 1984:15–18).

Several points need to be made. Native speakers are generally not aware of the vast number of sounds they produce (e.g., the aspirated initial voiceless stop in American English). That vast number is subject to scientific study, by phonetics. (See figure 5.1.) Natural spoken languages contain phonemes in their sound systems. Every natural language can be most efficiently written with the correct roster of phonemes.[6] Once the phonetic rules for producing phonemes in a given natural language are mastered, one can correctly pronounce a language written phonemically.

Scientific analysis of the phonological system of a natural language reveals structure that the native speaker is a master of and can produce at will but is usually not aware of. The phonological analysis is logically prior to the morphemic and syntactic analysis.

Speech Sounds: Scientific Empirical Observation Language

By the middle of the twentieth century we had an observation language, the IPA, and we had a theory for the structure of sounds in spoken language (the phoneme). The descriptive problem is to be able to perceive and record the hundreds of sounds actually made in the course of speech. The solution is the IPA, which can be presented as a chart.

This empirical observation language is concerned with the sounds of speech. The major analytic segments are the phone, the syllable, and the suprasegmentals, such as pitch and loudness, which co-occur with the phones and syllables but co-occur over more than one of them.

The IPA is constructed as a model of the vocal tract, and this kind of phonetic analysis is articulatory as opposed to acoustic.[7] The vocal tract has been analytically divided into parts: mouth, tongue, thorax, nasal passage. Among the dimensions are place where the sound is articulated (lips, teeth, palate, uvula), whether the breath is going out or coming in, whether the vocal cords are vibrating, whether the sound is continuous or stopped, and so forth. Every phone manifests at least some of these dimensions.

Each phone manifests a number of dimensions simultaneously. The [t] in the word *stop*, for example, is voiceless, a stop, and the point of articulation is the alveolar ridge (the tip of the tongue hits the roof of the mouth where it joins the upper front teeth). In contrast, the [d] in *dip* is voiced, a stop, and the point of articulation is the alveolar ridge. Vowels are voiced, continuous, and characterized by the conformation of the tongue in the mouth. In the [I] as in *teeth*, for example, the mouth is organized so that the articulation is high, front, and unrounded. For the [u] in *moose*, on the other hand, it is low, back, and rounded.

In a scientific observation language one goal is that dimensions be monothetic and be defined independently of each other. There must be no conflation of one dimension with another in the definitions.

Each of these phonetic dimensions is defined independently of the others. Efforts are made to increase the likelihood that they are monothetic. They are the "same kind of thing" because they are anchored in a natural constant, the anatomy of the human vocal tract. Voiced versus voiceless is produced by vibration of the vocal cords in a stream of air. This is the same thing no matter who produces it and no matter what natural language it is produced in.

THE INTERNATIONAL PHONETIC ALPHABET (revised to 2005)

CONSONANTS (PULMONIC)   © 2005 IPA

	Bilabial	Labiodental	Dental	Alveolar	Postalveolar	Retroflex	Palatal	Velar	Uvular	Pharyngeal	Glottal
Plosive	p b			t d		ʈ ɖ	c ɟ	k ɡ	q ɢ		ʔ
Nasal	m	ɱ		n		ɳ	ɲ	ŋ	ɴ		
Trill	ʙ			r					ʀ		
Tap or Flap				ⱱ		ɽ					
Fricative	ɸ β	f v	θ ð	s z	ʃ ʒ	ʂ ʐ	ç ʝ	x ɣ	χ ʁ	ħ ʕ	h ɦ
Lateral fricative				ɬ ɮ							
Approximant		ʋ		ɹ		ɻ	j	ɰ			
Lateral approximant				l		ɭ	ʎ	ʟ			

Where symbols appear in pairs, the one to the right represents a voiced consonant. Shaded areas denote articulations judged impossible.

CONSONANTS (NON-PULMONIC)

Clicks	Voiced implosives	Ejectives
ʘ Bilabial	ɓ Bilabial	' Examples:
ǀ Dental	ɗ Dental/alveolar	p' Bilabial
ǃ (Post)alveolar	ʄ Palatal	t' Dental/alveolar
ǂ Palatoalveolar	ɠ Velar	k' Velar
ǁ Alveolar lateral	ʛ Uvular	s' Alveolar fricative

OTHER SYMBOLS

ʍ Voiceless labial-velar fricative
w Voiced labial-velar approximant
ɥ Voiced labial-palatal approximant
ʜ Voiceless epiglottal fricative
ʢ Voiced epiglottal fricative
ʡ Epiglottal plosive

ɕ ʑ Alveolo-palatal fricatives
ɺ Voiced alveolar lateral flap
ɧ Simultaneous ʃ and x

Affricates and double articulations
can be represented by two symbols
joined by a tie bar if necessary.

k͡p t͡s

VOWELS

Where symbols appear in pairs, the one to the right represents a rounded vowel.

SUPRASEGMENTALS

ˈ Primary stress
ˌ Secondary stress   ˌfoʊnəˈtɪʃən
ː Long   eː
ˑ Half-long   eˑ
˘ Extra-short   ĕ
| Minor (foot) group
‖ Major (intonation) group
. Syllable break ɹi.ækt
‿ Linking (absence of a break)

DIACRITICS   Diacritics may be placed above a symbol with a descender, e.g. ŋ̊

̥ Voiceless	n̥ d̥	̤ Breathy voiced	b̤ a̤	̪ Dental	t̪ d̪	
̬ Voiced	s̬ t̬	̰ Creaky voiced	b̰ a̰	̼ Apical	t̺ d̺	
ʰ Aspirated	tʰ dʰ	̪ Linguolabial	t̼ d̼	̺ Laminal	t̻ d̻	
̹ More rounded	ɔ̹	ʷ Labialized	tʷ dʷ	̃ Nasalized	ẽ	
̜ Less rounded	ɔ̜	ʲ Palatalized	tʲ dʲ	ⁿ Nasal release	dⁿ	
̟ Advanced	u̟	ˠ Velarized	tˠ dˠ	ˡ Lateral release	dˡ	
̠ Retracted	e̠	ˤ Pharyngealized	tˤ dˤ	̚ No audible release	d̚	
̈ Centralized	ë	̴ Velarized or pharyngealized	ɫ			
̽ Mid-centralized	e̽	̝ Raised	e̝ (ɹ̝ = voiced alveolar fricative)			
̩ Syllabic	n̩	̞ Lowered	e̞ (β̞ = voiced bilabial approximant)			
̯ Non-syllabic	e̯	̘ Advanced Tongue Root	e̘			
̴ Rhoticity	ɚ a˞	̙ Retracted Tongue Root	e̙			

TONES AND WORD ACCENTS

LEVEL		CONTOUR	
e̋ or ꜛ	Extra high	ě or ꜛ	Rising
é ꜛ	High	ê ꜛ	Falling
ē ꜛ	Mid	e᷄ ꜛ	High rising
è ꜛ	Low	e᷅ ꜛ	Low rising
ȅ ꜛ	Extra low	e᷈ ꜛ	Rising-falling
↓ Downstep		↗ Global rise	
↑ Upstep		↘ Global fall	

Figure 5.1. Courtesy of the International Phonetic Association.

In the case of phonetics, the values on the dimensions are represented in the phonetic symbols. Some symbols represent a combination of dimensions (as [t]). Some values on dimensions are represented uniquely (as in ∧ or ~). Variation in the phones can be represented with diacritical marks (for length, nasalization, etc.).

The scale type of each dimension is known. Relative pitch, volume, and length are ordinal scales. The position of articulation, or the location of the tongue for the vowels, is probably nominal, although the underlying dimension is a continuum. Some of those positions are more or less fixed (bilabial, uvular), although each of them can be modified by front and back. Air stream is either stopped or continuant, which is a nominal scale.

The lexicon for representing each possibility on each dimension is by now a sign such as p, >, or ~. Numbers are not used. Each is unambiguous, for each is unique, an effort which is supported by actions of the International Phonetic Association.

There is no device for aiding observation. Training is then critically important. A large amount of the training takes place in practice sessions, and frequently a seasoned expert is working alongside the trainee. In the United States the linguistics profession runs a summer institute where scholars from all over the world teach courses, give lectures, or just hang out, and students come to be trained. It involves intensive training in the standards of the discipline, including how to observe, record, and reproduce speech sounds.

The experience of generations of linguists has been the proof of the pudding. The *International Journal of American Linguistics*, for example, specializes in the non–Indo-European languages of the Western Hemisphere. Every issue contains articles which describe the phonology of some language or some set of languages. Through the vast experience of the authors, readers, and editors of this journal it would by now be obvious if there were serious difficulties with the IPA. The only rational conclusion is that, as practice, the IPA works, and it works in a broadly comparative framework.

The IPA is not (yet) a perfect empirical observation language. Semantic drift has not been brought under firm control. In their 1986 book, Pullum and Ladusaw present versions of the IPA as well as American phonetic alphabets (1986:256–266). They state: "When linguistic transcriptions are presented, they should be accompanied by a note stating clearly which transcription system has been used, with detailed notes on any unusual or potentially ambiguous symbols" (Pullum and Ladusaw 1986:xxx). If this reminds the reader of the necessity to provide the scale along with the number in reporting temperature prior to the adoption of SI, it should.

There is another more serious problem with the IPA, detailed in Ladefoged and Halle (1988). The IPA was based on segments of sound, and by the third trimester of the twentieth century it had become clear that features were at least as important as segments (Ladefoged and Halle, 1988:577). Following on the work of Roman Jakobson, generative phonology has come to focus on a number of dimensions of sound called features (see Roca and Johnson 1999). The phone and the syllable are segments of the sound stream, and the IPA does a good job of isolating the segments. But each phone is composed of values on a dimension (voicing, place of articulation, nasalization, etc.), and the stream of sound can be viewed as simultaneous streams of dimensions. Generative phonologists are actively working on this system of dimensions and how these dimensions interact with each other (see Roca and Johnson 1999:630–664). The number of dimensions (features) is in flux, as are their definitions.

Ladefoged and Halle in 1988 argued that the IPA should be changed to reflect the new understanding of phonological behavior, although they recognized that it would not be easy to accomplish.

A convention to revise the IPA alphabet was called for the summer of 1989 in Kiel, Germany (the call appeared in the July 1989 issue of the journal *Phonetica*). According to Ladefoged, the convention assembled, working groups met, a revised IPA resulted, and it was voted on the by the Council of the International Phonetic Association (1990). Ladefoged reports that perhaps no one was satisfied with the result and urges continual work on the problem.

Here we have an effort to consciously control the empirical observation language which is not as mature as the SI system. It reminds one more of the biological taxonomies, although it is not yet as mature. The reasons include some unresolved theoretical issues and a (consequent?) lack of consensus on the need for a single solution. A puzzle in all of these cases is the nature of the imperative to use the "official" system in public communications. What encourages, or forces, editors and publishers to adopt a single standard?

The IPA is not part of a natural language or culture. While it originated in the West it is not a part of some Western natural culture. It is a scientific system. It stresses uniqueness, single dimensions, known scale types, self-conscious calibration efforts when crossing boundaries, and self-conscious replication and testing of descriptions. These features separate it from natural culture and language, and do so decisively.[8]

Object

What is the object where the phonological dimensions are manifest? We start with a spoken natural language, which has sounds (>600), phonemes (10–120), morphemes (>1,000), words (many thousands), syntax, semantics, and discourse. All (spoken) natural languages have these properties

(Witkowski 1996). Naturally occurring speech events (a stream of sounds) manifest the natural language.

We can (and do) analyze that stream of speech into components. The object is, then, that stream of speech in a natural language. We can easily find examples of that object in speech communities. We can of course also find it elsewhere (e.g., in major cities in other countries, on airplanes, on radio and TV broadcasts, etc.).

Sometimes we set up special interactions, called interviews, to elicit certain kinds of behavior in what is not a natural setting.[9] When working on an unfamiliar language it is hard to do phonological analysis of natural interaction. It goes far too fast, at least at first. The interview allows one to slow things down, and to go over a particular point many times. But given the nature of language (native speakers have control over that language and can produce that language in virtually any setting), the interview does not constitute a plausible challenge to the validity of the analysis.

We try to give unambiguous names to the objects, the different natural languages. "English" and "Hindi" are names of languages, and there is little ambiguity. We know something about approximately more than seven thousand natural languages (Grimes, 1996; Witkowski 1996). I do not know if the names of the natural languages have the property of uniqueness.

We have before us an example of a very successful scientific empirical observation procedure for dealing with structure and variation in a human cultural behavior. The subject matter of this system, the structure of the sounds humans make while speaking, is not inherently a part of any natural culture meaning system. The structure of speech is in almost every case part of what Sapir called unconscious culture. There is no evidence that more than a very few individuals are aware of phonological or grammatical structure. This is in clear contrast to ways to find and kill game, the selection of rice varieties for planting in a field, or the timing of a trading expedition. In these latter cases the choices are made after much discussion of the choices and the reasons for the choices. In contradistinction the choices made in phonological structure are virtually never conscious and virtually never discussed.[10]

In the case of phonology the dimensions are approaching singularity, the language for expressing the values of dimensions has achieved uniqueness (if not universal agreement), the scale types are known, the concepts are based on universally distributed natural phenomena, and training is systematic and widespread. One observation language, the IPA, is without significant ambiguity, has unique names, and is devoid of cultural bias. There is a convention that addresses issues of meaning and use of the lexical items in the language. The object is also clear: the production of streams of speech of a natural language. Analysis of the phonological subsystem has now achieved a wide consensus.

This observational language meets all of the criteria for any scientific observation language—it has reduced ambiguity to virtually zero, cultural contamination has been eliminated, and semantic drift is coming under conventional social control. I claim to have demonstrated that we have achieved a scientific empirical observation language for one aspect of culture1.

Notes

1. A natural language is one spoken in a speech community (where high levels of mutual intelligibility hold), and it is learned by its speakers as infants and children, with no more than occasional formal training.

2. The target language is not one's own but the other language(s) one is trying to study and learn.

3. A stop is a consonant in which the air stream is interrupted, or stopped. Examples include [p, b, t, d, k, g].

4. I thank Shukti Chaudhuri-Brill for this example.

5. I thank Nitish Jha for these pairs.

6. American Sign Language is a natural language, but it is not a spoken language. It has morphology, syntax, and semantics but obviously no phonic system and therefore no phonemes. There are at most a handful of nonspoken natural languages in the world, whereas the figure of seven thousand natural spoken languages seems to be a reasonable approximation (see Grimes, 1996).

7. Articulatory phonetics represent the movements made in producing the sounds. These movements take place in the vocal tract. Acoustic phonetics is the study of the physics of the sound stream.

8. It is not known to me the degree to which the evolution of the system was driven by a conscious knowledge of scientific observation criteria. It may have been that the development of scientific measurement was "in the air" in the nineteenth century and that the early phoneticians were aware of these matters. On the other hand it may be that this is a case of independent invention.

9. There is a substantial literature on reactive versus nonreactive measures. It is clear, for example, that on some topics the age and sex of the interviewer has an effect on the information recorded. Every phonologist knows that the interview situation is special and knows how to calibrate between interviews and natural settings. There are some who say that any question, any interview, any interaction changes the situation, and therefore the information. Such assertions are only very rarely backed up with evidence for the effect.

10. Those who have been exposed to instruction in grammar in school or who read William Safire (or Fowler) may disagree with this. It is my experience that the vast majority of literate persons in this world (until very recently a very tiny percentage of all persons) are not capable of engaging in an extended discussion of such choices or the reasoning involved in making any such choice. Many people can hear differences; few even among the educated are capable of discussing the reasoning involved.

CHAPTER SIX

~

Ethnobiology

Ethnoscience has come to refer to the study of the knowledge held within natural cultures. There are many plausible topics to study in this domain, including disease, soils, weather, dreams, human power relationships, and flora and fauna. The topic that has received the most attention is the systematics of macroflora and -fauna. Ethnobiology, particularly ethnobotany, has been the subject of considerable scientific curiosity, due in part to the European search for economically and pharmacologically useful plants and plant substances. Systematic study of these domains seems to be a post–World War II phenomenon (Hunn 1996).

Ethnoscience is well equipped to investigate systems of native or folk meanings which are strongly represented in the natural language lexicon. Among the easier realms to deal with are those with a material referent (e.g., colors, plants, animals, astronomy, soils) and where the substance of that material is also the subject of scientific study.[1] When this latter is the case, there is a scientific understanding of the subject which is independent of the native understanding.[2]

Harold Conklin was one of the first to succeed in doing a study of this sort. His Hanunóo book, on shifting cultivators in the Philippines, contained a detailed study of the plants that the Hanunóo recognized, named, and used (1957). Conklin was responsible not only for the Hanunóo material but also for the plant identification, apparently doing both identifications himself. Furthermore, he specified where most of the plants were found and how they were used, all in the context of a study of Hanunóo shifting agriculture and social organization. It was not primarily a study of Hanunóo semantics or of the principles of Hanunóo plant classification, but it was a magnificent study of some aspects of Hanunóo knowledge of their physical and botanical environment.

Conklin showed that a relatively small and simple society had very detailed knowledge of at least some aspects of their environment. This was not surprising in itself, but the number of plants named and used was, in retrospect, rather high (sixteen hundred plants named in Hanunóo, representing some twelve hundred Linnaean plants [Conklin 1957:44]).[3]

These early efforts were followed by a number of cultural ecology studies in the highlands of New Guinea, of which Rappaport's *Pigs for the Ancestors* (1968) is the most famous. In these studies the flow of energy to and from humans is the major consideration, but Rappaport was interested in identifying the plants used by the Tsembaga Maring and what the nutritional and end-use characteristics of those plants were. He focused not so much on Tsembaga knowledge of those plants but on Tsembaga use of those plants. To find out what the plants and their properties were, he collected them and had them analyzed in a scientific framework. He did not ask what the Tsembaga understanding of those plants was. His was a heroic effort. The amount of data collected was very large and required an effort both arduous and sustained. Criticisms of an incompatibility of his research design with his thesis are probably warranted. Criticisms of his data collection are wide of the mark.

By far the most elaborate project in ethnoscience is that of Brent Berlin and his associates. Volumes on Tzeltal plant classification (Berlin, Breedlove, and Raven 1974) and Tzeltal animal classification (Hunn 1977) have appeared. Berlin et al. 1974 is a study of the plants named by some speakers of Tzeltal and of the principles of plant classification, all compared with systematic scientific study of collections of the same plants and a study of the principles used in the scientific system. It is a comparison (among other things) of two systems of plant classification.

As noted in chapter 4, biological systematics is not merely another specialized facet of Western natural culture. It is a fully developed analytic observation procedure, with calibration in nature, monothetic dimensions, and unambiguous terminology for representing observations. It is scientific culture, not natural culture. In ethnobiology we have material objects (the plants and animals), which are specified in a scientific empirical observation language. Berlin's team also collected, systematically, the Tzeltal lexicon which names those very same plants. The scientific framework is defined independently of the Tzeltal framework. We know that if there is congruence between the two systems of classification it is not due to contamination by tautologies in the definitions.

One of the more interesting results of the Berlin et al. studies is that there is an enormous amount of correlation between the two classifications. Furthermore, there is relatively little ambiguity in the Tzeltal terminology. Apparently the uniqueness of naming rule is adhered to in this realm of the Tzeltal lexicon.

We have in this case the simultaneous use of two sets of scientific observation procedures, linguistics and taxonomy. Linguistics is used to observe, describe, and analyze the linguistic utterances; taxonomy is used to observe, describe, and analyze the biological specimens.

At the heart of this question is one of expertise. Every scientific procedure has the built-in assumption of replication. The correctness of the results of the application of a procedure is measured by how well it correlates with some other application of the same procedure. What is often overlooked in all this is the proper training and proper carrying out of the procedure. Errors in training or application will hopefully cause different results.[4]

Experts, who are by definition well trained and apply procedures with great care and diligence, are presumed to get results reasonably free from error. But science generally will not accept the results of only one expert. If no one else can get the same results, they are said not to be replicated, and it is usual to conclude that there are significant errors somewhere. Validity in science is a product of a correlation—a result is valid if it correlates very highly with another result, either a standard that is accepted by all workers in the field or with the results of at least one other expert.[5]

Establishing that standard is a critical part of science, and one that has become almost invisible to even most scientists. The National Institute of Standards and Technology is responsible for creating and maintaining many such standards in the United States. The operating rule in science is that no single expert is authoritative—at least two must be able to get the same results before the validity of the results is accepted.

Berlin et al. did raise the question of agreement of experts. What they found is very interesting but has not been explored. For the Tzeltal plant study they used three primary informants, plus another ten used less intensively, and worked with these informants for what must have been many hundreds of hours. They collected fifteen thousand different plants and had at least five examples of each one. At higher levels of the taxonomy, they found very little disagreement among their informants on which name went with which plant. But at lower levels, for some sorts of plants they found a great deal of difference of opinion, and they report that their informants would discuss this situation for hours. Berlin et al. mention this in passing and do not write as if it was the focus of any substantial analysis. And yet the situation is pregnant with interest. Is it the case that natural culture taxonomies have areas or zones of uncertainty or free choice? Or is it the case that experts in the natural culture have limited areas of expertise, and therefore one job of the outside analyst is to identify and locate the boundaries of expertise? Or might it be the case that Berlin et al.'s informants were not uniformly expert? There is much for the cognitive scientist to ponder.

For the study of ethnobiology, then, we are dealing with how a natural culture names discrete biological items (organisms) in its environment. For that study we use two scientific observation procedures: linguistics for observing, recording, and analyzing the terms and the relationship of the terms and the objects in the natural language, and taxonomy for observing, recording, and analyzing the organisms and their relationships. Then the two measures are correlated. A further step, analyzing the Tzeltal principles of classification, is performed on the results of the linguistic and taxonomic procedures and their correlation.

The scientific observation languages that apply are already worked out and have been given as examples: taxonomy and linguistics.[6] The objects and dimensions are in existence, and comparability has been established.

The Social Object Problem

In most scientific studies the dimensions are in focus, and the objects are secondary (although necessary). In ethnobiology we are observing the classification of plants and animals in a natural culture. The lowest-level objects are relatively unproblematic in this case, due in large part to there being long traditions for both linguistics and taxonomy.

There is a generic problem with the highest-level objects. It has been claimed that the ethnobotany and ethnozoology of "Tzeltal" has been observed and published. Tzeltal "natural culture" is the highest-level object. When we assert that dimensions of human life are associated with each other, as correlation or cause and effect, we are arguing that systems of these dimensions exist. But that system must be manifest someplace in reality. The usual locus for that system is what is usually labeled language, community, culture, society, or nation. But the next step, modification of culture and so on with singular pronouns (a, the), is profoundly problematic. By this simple linguistic act we state that particular, singular, identifiable, and discernable languages, cultures, and societies exist. If we are to be serious about this move, then we must have operations that identify a particular culture and differentiate it from others.

In the case of modern nation-states, this is rarely a problem. Such states usually have clear borders, and any given spatial locus is either inside or outside the unit. Furthermore, there are a few institutions which cover the whole territory (central bank, currency, customs laws, census, etc.). Knowing the identity and location of the state for any given space is rarely a problem in the twentieth century.

There is little justification for assuming that this model of territorial exclusivity can be extended to other kinds of social organization. Modern Europeans usually draw maps of languages and other societies with lines between them. This implies that there are clear borders to such languages and societies, by analogy with modern nation-states. Not only is there little justification presented for such an allegation, there is substantial evidence that it does not correspond to the facts on the ground (Berndt 1959, 1976; Hymes 1968).

In the modern era there are several dimensions of culture1 which are manifest in each individual. They include at least dialect(s) and language(s) spoken, religion, ethnicity, class, race, education, and vocation. It is perfectly clear that virtually no modern nation-state shows a perfect correlation of all of these factors with the national territory. For example, there are chains of dialects that cross national borders and which challenge the notion of "a language" and the correlation of a nation and a language (cf. Hymes [1968] for a particularly clear and trenchant presentation). If they are not perfectly correlated, then the nation as object does not map the distribution of dimensions perfectly.

The more general problem of the culture-bearing unit has been discussed since Tylor's first comparative paper in 1889 (see Lagace 1967). The Naroll-Moerman debate clarified many of the issues, but no clear theoretical conclusion was reached (Naroll 1964, 1968, 1970a; Moerman 1965, 1968b).

If a system of dimensions (a set of correlated variables) is to exist, then its relationship to a national boundary is the problem, not the solution. Where on the ground are we to find systems of variables, and with what sort of "object" do those systems correlate? The territory or group with which they correlate becomes the locus of the system. But if that territory or group is problematic, what has happened to our system? Where do we go to find it? And in any empirical study we must have a place to go to find it.

The work that is needed on this matter is to observe, for each substantive case, where the system is to be found. Culture, society, community are metaphors, not solutions. And when we talk of a culture, or a society, we are imputing a system where one has not as yet been demonstrated.

The only program (I know of) which has even begun to face this question is the striking suggestion of Przeworski and Teune that true comparative analysis will operate with several levels of analysis at once (1970). Their solution is to gather data from many different individuals, from many different households, from many different communities, from many different cultures (they say nations). In the analysis one looks for order at each level of analysis. If the national level accounts for some of the variance, then to that degree the nation is a system. If a community accounts for some of the variance, then the community is to that degree a system. One can imagine that the empirical results would challenge the assumptions of systems at social levels that we all operate with. As far as I know, no one has ever put this expensive and arduous program into effect.

When Murdock and his colleagues set out to prepare a 186-culture subsample of the Standard Cross Cultural Sample (SCCS), they were in part responding to the problems of social objects (Murdock and White 1969). In most past efforts in anthropological large-sample comparisons, the names of cultures are taken as the sampling units. Such cultures are on occasion studied by more than one person, at more than one place, and at more than one time.

The basis for treating all such accounts as referring to the "same" unit is based on the unit having the same name. However, the assignment of a name to a culture is often an arbitrary procedure. Occasionally the same name will be given to two cultures. Equally often the same culture will receive two or more names. Obviously this produces chaos for the sampling procedure. The Murdock and White solution was to focus their smaller sample on work in a single location, usually a community, and at a single point in time. This neatly does away with many kinds of uncertainty. But it does nothing to enable us to work on the problem of the contribution of levels of analysis to accounting for variance in dimensional correlations. This strategy, in other words, will not help us toward using the Przeworski and Teune suggestion for solving the problem of system location.

We have, it appears, considerable uncertainty regarding the identity of the object (society, culture) that manifests our dimensions. At the same time, we have discovered a substantial number of interlocked correlations of dimensions (Naroll 1970b; Goody 1976; Levinson and Malone 1980; Johnson and Earle 1987; Ember and Levinson 1991). The large number of correlations must indicate that some kinds of systems exist.

Most (but by no means all) of the loci for the observations (by anthropologists) have been small in scale (the site of fieldwork, by and large, as captured by the Murdock and White sample). This must mean that these small-scale loci exhibit some systemic properties. As an object, then, these small-scale locales work for comparative studies trying to correlate variables. What is not clear is whether there is any justification for generalizing from these small-scale loci to any larger objects implied by the terms "culture" and "society." The Przeworski and Teune program would answer the question. The problem deserves much more effort.

It has been demonstrated that there is scientific empirical observation of meaning behavior in a natural culture. Two scientific observation languages—linguistics and taxonomy—have been applied to events in natural cultures. Each of the observation languages is well developed, and training in using them is readily available. Problems of ambiguity in the observation languages have largely been solved. The observers came in two batches—experts in linguistics and the natural culture and experts in taxonomy—and they have to work together. This division of labor is not necessary, but few individuals will achieve sufficient training in both to be effective. There are material constants which are referents for both observation languages, so they are calibrated.[7] The problems of ambiguity and cultural contamination have been solved, and this strategy for cross-cultural research no longer seems to contain problems of comparability of dimensions. The object, in contrast, remains problematic.

Notes

1. If the subject is ideas about gods, or magic, or dreams, it is much harder to be specific and clear about the referents of the native lexical categories.

2. The other side of the coin, of course, is that native expertise in some domain, such as plant classification, must be matched by analyst expertise in the domain. It is a rare anthropologist who can claim this expertise. The strategy of choice then will usually be an interdisciplinary team. This means taking two or more analysts to the field, probably for extended periods of time, and it is not easy to get a practicing specialist in, say, soil science, to spend several months in some very small, remote place with few industrial facilities and worrisome health conditions. The practical constraints on doing this kind of work are very great indeed.

3. Other efforts to study agriculture—for example, Freeman's very useful study of Iban shifting agriculture—had focused on labor inputs and scheduling. Freeman mentions that some (unspecified) catch crops were grown at the edge of the swiddens (1955). Freeman clearly was not very interested in the plants the Iban used, nor was he interested in Iban knowledge of the plants in their environment.

4. It is entirely possible that errors in the procedure can cause a replication, whereas an error-free procedure will prevent a replication. We confidently predict that errors in procedures will cause results to differ, not to coincide, and in most cases that is a justified confidence. But it is not a certainty.

5. Establishing the authority of an expert, and the process for so doing, is not altogether transparent. Community consensus is probably often a factor, but then we need to tease out what leads a community to achieve consensus on this matter. Goodenough relies on the concept of the native expert (in *Description and Comparison* [1970]) but does not tell us in any detail how they or we are to recognize such persons.

6. I have here shifted from the demonstration that phonology is a social science to an assertion that linguistics warrants the same status. What is at issue here is the identification of lexicon and of items in the lexicon. There will be problems with "word" and "a word," but my sense is that they are reasonably trivial problems. I think my assertion about "linguistics" is reasonable in this context.

7. There are many interpretive issues that deserve further thought. One is the sampling of informants. Can we generalize from the Berlin et al. sample of informants to any wider set of individuals? The answer to that is unknown. Their informants were generally younger men who worked as farmers. Would, say, women, older men, and traders have the same knowledge? Would any sample of young men give the same performances? How much variation is there within the population? These are all fascinating and important questions. But they are not questions of empirical observation. They are instead questions of research design, such as the sampling frame. This book is confined to solving the problems of empirical observation technology, and I contend that in this Tzeltal case these problems have been solved.

CHAPTER SEVEN

∽

Labor Productivity in Agriculture

The amount of energy expended in the quest for food by animals is a major concern in several different fields. For humans, Sahlins (1972) and Lee (1988) have argued that hunters and gatherers (henceforth foragers) are the original affluent society, for they have to spend very few hours per day in the food quest, and fewer by far than an agriculturalist. In the same vein Boserup has argued that as preindustrial agriculture intensifies, the output per hour of work declines (1965). Labor productivity is thus a major concern in thinking about mammalian ecology, about the evolution of human society, and about agricultural development.

There are major disagreements in the literature on how human labor productivity varies with the evolution of social complexity. The pessimists claim increases in agricultural technology lower the productivity of labor (Boserup 1965). For example, some claim that the productivity of swidden systems is higher than the productivity of permanent fields (Carneiro 1961; Boserup 1965; Sahlins 1972). Others have held that agricultural productivity, and especially labor productivity, rises along with the shift from long-fallow to permanent-field regimes (Harris 1979; Ellen 1982; Bronson 1972). There are good theoretical reasons to investigate agricultural (and more generally food production) labor productivity.

The measurement of labor productivity[1] in the food system is in consequence an important activity, and it is productive to take a careful look at the conceptual and observation problems.

There are three major types of human plant food production systems: for-aging where no domesticated species are consumed; horticulture where there may well be hundreds of species, intercropping, and continuous production; and agriculture dependent primarily upon one or a few major seasonal grass crops. There have been a handful of empirical studies of the labor produc-tivity of foragers (see Lee and DeVore 1968; Leacock and Lee 1982; and In-gold, Riches, and Woodburn 1988). There have also been a number of de-tailed studies of horticulturalists (e.g., Rappaport 1968; Bayliss-Smith 1982; Ellen 1982).

Three grass systems now dominate in world agriculture: rice, maize, and wheat-barley. There have been a very large number of empirical studies of agriculture, focusing particularly on rice, and some have been done of maize systems. There are virtually none of wheat-barley systems (but see Russell 1988). Cassava, sweet potatoes, and yams have received some attention. A scientific observation system must be clear about the dimensions that are to be observed and about the objects which manifest those dimensions. In the case of agricultural productivity the "object" is the system of behavior that results in organic products that can be used as food for the human group that acquires them. The dimensions include land area, technology, labor input, and food output.

The object, at least as it occurs in small scale (as in a farm, or a set of farms in a community), is not problematic. We start with a natural culture, and then move down to a locality, and in that locality look for the operations which produce the food.

The dimensions are not without their problems. A necessary dimension for the study of agricultural productivity is crop output. No measure of rela-tive efficiency can exist without measures of output. But the dimension on which we can measure output is not clear. Ideally we would have a single di-mension that all the various outputs (crops) share, and that dimension should not distort our understanding of the particular agricultural systems.

Many ecologists would have us measure energy as the output variable. En-ergy would do for grains and potatoes but would seriously distort our under-standing of cabbage, lettuce, and cucumbers and would not account for chili peppers, sweet basil, and cotton at all.

The economists would have us measure output in monetary terms. This is at best an indirect measure (because there are many sources of variation in price, including quality, national subsidies, and international exchange ra-tios). But more important, not all agricultural systems participate in pricing their output. If there is no market for the output there is no uncontested way to assign a monetary value. Neither energy nor money is acceptable as a dimension for measuring the output of very different agricultural systems. An empirical investigation of the input–output ratios of different kinds of agricultural systems is therefore not possible, at least at the moment.

What we can do is compare the same crop produced under different conditions (different technology, different soils, different land tenure regimes, etc.). Using this strategy, the output can be defined in volume (liters), mass (kilograms), or caloric terms. Because only one crop is used, the results are far more comparable across the particular instances. This chapter will focus on rice. We have by far the most studies of rice agriculture of any agricultural system, we have covered more of the range of technologies, and we understand it the best as a system. As a result the successes and problems with empirical measurement are in better focus than with the other cropping systems (Hunt 2000).

With rice agriculture the object is quite clear. Rice is a grass widely grown in Asia, and under many different conditions, including hill swiddens, on terraces, and on lowland floodplains. It is grown as both a dry-foot[2] and wet-foot crop. Most rice systems in Southeast Asia involve a cult of a rice goddess, so there is a great deal of attention paid to the system by the participants. There is no doubt that rice agriculture exists, and is the same kind of thing whenever it occurs in Asia.

The primary dimensions to be observed in investigating agricultural labor productivity are (1) land area utilized, (2) genetic material (crop), (3) technology, (4) labor effort, and (5) output (see Moran 1995; Hunt 1995, 2000). Some of these are observed with dimensions that are close to being fully formed variables. We are still early in the evolutionary development of some others.

Land Area

This refers to the extent of the area that is cropped.[3] There are possible complications, for a larger area is typically cleared than is planted. This can be specified, and if it is not there is some uncertainty introduced. Area is thus not ambiguous, nor is land. But the observer should specify exactly how the land area is defined. In this case we have solid quantitative measurement. The scale type is ratio. The scale values are numbers, and so there should be no ambiguity in the scale units. The observation language is SI.

Crop

The general notion here is that a kind of a plant is being cultivated, and which crops are being cultivated are to be specified (observed). Some crops are clearly and totally domesticated (maize is one, the date palm another), and most of what we call crops are domesticated, planted, tended, and then harvested by humans. (There are some marginal cases, such as wild fruit trees that are protected, pruned, fertilized, etc.) For a study of productivity in the food system, these shadings from domesticated to wild would need explicit and careful attention. In this case, rice agriculture, the problem is far less severe.

The dimension, crop, is named in the natural culture and is also identified in the scientific taxonomy. The likelihood of ambiguity, or cultural contamination, is very low.[4]

The dimension is reasonably close to being monothetic. Each individual crop plant is identified and named.

The scale type is nominal, with all the attendant problems with ambiguity in the lexicon of the scale values. The major problem will come in the lexicon used to name the scale values. In the crudest case the genus being grown is named and is normally identified with a word, such as *rice* or *yam*. Traditional rice farmers in Asia plant from five to fifteen different varieties in their farms and may know of sixty or more (Janlekha 1955; Freeman 1955; Conklin 1957). Conklin reports that the Ifugao have an elaborate taxonomy for naming these varieties (personal communication).

Clearly, then, the crop variety that is grown can be identified in the natural and in the scientific taxonomies. At the level of "rice," or "bean," there is virtually no opportunity for ambiguity. The observation language is the Linnaean taxonomy.

Technology

I prefer a broad definition of technology; in the case of food systems it would include plants, animals, tools, knowledge, and practices. Many of these are monothetic dimensions.[5]

The literature on agricultural productivity uses only a few of the aspects of technology. Technology is usually perceived as a package of tools and practices, and these are named as length of fallow (long to multiple cropping), techniques of field preparation (fire, plowing), whether there is irrigation, and techniques of sowing (dibbling, broadcasting, transplanting in the case of rice).[6] These various dimensions are named in words and seem to have stable meanings across scholars and natural cultures.

Fallow time is the length of time that a field is not under cultivation. It is badly named. It usually refers to the frequency of cropping in a solar year and can vary from as high as eight or nine (in the cases of vegetables like radishes) to 0.04 (once every twenty-five years). Therefore none of these refers to fallow. It should be renamed as frequency of cropping of a given area of land, it should specify annuals or perennials, and the time frame should be as long as the longest crop cycle (possibly Chicozapote in Mexico, with a bearing life of 250 years). Under this circumstance the cropping frequency would range from one (per 250 years) to two thousand (eight per year, for 250 years).

Associated with frequency of cropping are field-preparation techniques. When fallow lasts more than a few years, swidden (or slash and burn)[7] is the label. It refers to clearing vegetation by cutting, burning the dried plant remains, and then preparing the ground for seeding with a dibble stick. With permanent-field agriculture (fallow no longer than a year, or at most two, with little growth of woody vegetation during the fallow period), hoeing or plowing are the techniques most often applied. Permanent-field agriculture can utilize plowing, working the land with spades, or even no land preparation (as in low tillage in industrial agriculture).

In fact, there is confusion in our concepts. There are three quite different concepts: dealing with the vegetation which is on the land to be cultivated, techniques for working the soil itself, and the length of fallow time.

The vegetation in moist-area infrequent cropping (long-fallow) systems has very considerable biomass, and individual plants may be huge (as in trees forty-five meters tall and two meters in circumference). In slash and burn this vegetation is cut, dried, and then fired. In frequent-cropping situations there is typically very little vegetation left from the previous crop, and dealing with it requires little labor. Burning may be sufficient, or it may be dealt with as part of soil preparation. Before plowing can be used the tree stumps must be removed, a major investment of labor that does not have to be repeated. Finally, there is the matter of the length of fallow. Length of fallow responds to population pressure, market demand, and environmental moisture. Vegetation and soil management will relate to fallow time, but not in a simple way. The three concepts should be defined and observed independently of each other. The scales for vegetation and soil preparation are nominal, and the words for describing the activities (the scale steps) appear to raise few problems of ambiguity. The scale for frequency of crop cycle is a ratio, the units are a single crop cycle and a solar year, and the lexicon uses numbers.

Soil preparation ranges from the minimal one of dibbling (poking a small hole in the ground with a pointed stick, then putting the seeds in the hole), through various degrees of turning over some of the soil (with hoes, spades, or plows), to plowing, harrowing, and pulverizing all the soil. In addition, with wet rice there is a mechanical mixing of the mud which is called puddling, which can be done by man or beast. Plows are pulled by some traction device (occasionally by humans, usually by draft animals such as donkeys, mules, horses, oxen, water buffalo, camels, elephants) or by engines (external combustion, internal combustion) of a vast range of sizes. The scale is nominal, and the words for designating the scale steps again appear to raise few problems of ambiguity.

Tools are another aspect of this dimension of technology, and the objects are named with words. The word refers to a tangible item, made by humans, which is used to perform work. Among the kinds of work involved are cutting of vegetation (axes, machetes, knives, sickles, etc.), breaking soil (dibble stick or coa, spade, hoe, plow, harrow, seed drill), providing traction (human, domesticated animal, engine), and carrying things (bag, basket, cart). These in turn can be made from a variety of substances, such as wood, cloth, animal skin, stone, and metal. Each of these in turn can be composed of many different types (species of wood, kinds of cloth, species of animals, different metals). The scales are nominal, and the scale values are of course represented by words.

Since this realm of human experience has been of intense interest to many for millennia there seems not to be much confusion when it is talked about. If there is profound ambiguity to be found in this lexicon it is not apparent. There are physical referents to the objects (if not to processes). The objects can be drawn or photographed, and brought home and put in museums. There are type specimens. Cultural contamination seems not to be a problem.

Labor Effort

The concept of labor effort seems to be quite simple. It is widely applied in studies of human economies. Labor is a key factor of production for almost everybody, and one of the prime concepts for the Marxist approach to almost everything. One would expect to conclude that the dimension is clearly conceptualized, operationalized, and named. Labor effort is often thought of as time, and the scale type is a ratio scale. The scale units are usually hours, days, or years and are represented with numbers. There is no ambiguity here.

Unfortunately, there is a major problem with the dimension, and that is ensuring that the scope of the dimension is clearly conceived and identically defined from one study to another. This is almost never the case. At issue here is what is considered to be work and what is not. One might imagine that every activity of a human over twenty-four hours could be observed on a nominal scale and assigned to a single category, such as work, leisure, sleep, and so on. If, as is actually the case, it is possible for a human adult to do two or more things at once, such as hunt game, patrol the boundary of the territory to protect against encroachment, and look for the next place to open a swidden field, then we can conceive of partitioning the effort of that expedition into, say, 60 percent hunting, 30 percent protection, and 10 percent swidden reconnaissance. The total hours spent, then, would be disaggregated into hours for the several tasks.

It is also possible to consider that a human does work that is not directly related to the farm task, or even to the food system. Here we have to reckon with construction work on the dwelling site, repair work on that site, construction and repair of tools, gathering firewood, brewing beer for a ceremony, and on and on. If these are to be called work there should be a clear-cut definition of what is work and what is not. This is missing in the accounts of agricultural work effort.

Next, if what is being measured is the work spent only on farming and not work spent on hunting, house-building, and so forth, then a clear concept of the farming task, and what constitutes work in that task, is needed. This is also uniformly missing from the literature. What we get instead is the number of hours or days spent in the fields, as if all those hours were farming work and as if no other hours spent were farming work. The situation with respect to the measuring of work is in a very unhappy state.[8]

In the case of work input, then, there is a possible dimension which has a ratio scale but no clear definition. The probability of unreliable and invalid measures is uncomfortably high. It is also the case that some concentrated work would probably solve the problem. It is not hopeless, just messy. It needs a set of conferences of interested scholars to hammer out solutions.

Output

Output usually refers to the plant material which is captured by humans for use. Urban analysts tend to concentrate on the fruit of the plant, especially for grasses and legumes. In fact, the straw of the grasses may be useful, and for some plants the leaves are also useful. Which of these parts are included is up to the analyst, of course. Different problems may well dictate different solutions.

A major practical reason for concentrating on the rice fruit is that it is reasonably homogeneous, it is a major foodstuff for the growers and other consumers, and it is in the center of interest of most farmers.

The identification of this single output is quite easy, and there is a natural basis for calibrating the measures. The fruits/seeds are hard, storable, and rich in food that is good for humans, and they all come ripe at about the same time, so visualizing the harvest is easy. Most of the natural cultures that have such harvests recognize them, and recognize the variable amounts of the harvest. "Output" then will not be ambiguous if it is recognized that only one aspect of the utility of the plant is being observed. This output is called the harvest, or the yield. It is clear what we are talking about.

There are basically four choices for a dimension in the case of rice. Volume or mass terms are widespread in natural cultures and in the West. Two others are energy contained (as calories) and value in a market (in money). Ecologists and economists are most likely to use these latter two metrics. In either case a prior measure in volume or mass is necessary, and then a conversion from the primary to the target metric is necessary. There are of course problems of validity in generating the converted measures. From here on the discussion will be concerned only with mass and volume.

Mass and volume are measured with ratio scales, and there is no ambiguity in what the numbers mean. There is, however, considerable ambiguity concerning the object that is being measured. All grain is harvested with a considerable amount of dry matter (chaff for rice, wheat, and millet; cobs and leaves for maize). This dry matter is bulky, light in mass, and not directly consumed by humans. It is removed by humans before consumption of the grain.

In the rice world of Southeast Asia there are separate names for the grain in different stages of processing. One of the meanings of *paddy* is the grain after separation from the stalk and before threshing and winnowing. *Rice* is the usual translation of the words for the fruit/berry/seed after it has been threshed and winnowed. Three volumes of paddy reduce to about two volumes of rice. There is a 33 percent reduction in volume, but the reduction in mass is on the order of only 6 percent in this same process (Kundstadter, Chapman, and Sabhasri, 1978). If the output is being measured as volume, then, it is crucial to know what stage of the process is being measured. If instead mass is being measured, then the difference between the two stages, while not trivial, is far less important. There is a very large window for confusion and error here, and specifying what one is measuring, and how, is the only way to avoid it.

The dimension, crop output, is fairly clearly conceptualized, it can be named in an unambiguous way, the scale type is ratio, and the observations are expressed in numbers.

For the five dimensions that are being considered, the first four are usually measured directly, and the observation language can be used directly in subsequent analytic efforts. Little translation or transformation is required to make these observations useful in comparative studies. (I am leaving to one side the problem with the definition of work.) With the last dimension, output, there is a different situation. Almost every case studied so far has natural culture measures of field size and output. The Chinese measures are catty and mou, in Thailand tang and rai. Many case studies are reported in the measures of the natural culture of the place. In these cases the translations, and subsequent transformations into European natural measures, need careful consideration.

In the anthropological context, data for comparative study are always gathered in two phases: a primary observing context of original fieldwork (the first anthropological project) and a secondary phase where a (large) set of primary measurements are put into comparable form.

It is often easy for the ethnographer to get some idea of the amount of land which is harvested and the amount of the main starch crop which is harvested from it. Apparently most farmers are interested in how much land is in production and how much is harvested from it, and there are often native forms of measurement for those quantities.[9] Many farmers remember these figures, and in any case, if the fieldworker is present at harvest time they are fairly easy to observe. In consequence, if an ethnography is to present one measure, it will usually be volume or weight of output per unit of land. The empirical observation languages for field use are clear and fairly easy to operate (see Hunt 1995; Moran 1995).

Secondary measurements are necessary in order to use these several cases for a systematic comparative study. All the primary observations have to be translated into a common language. The measurement language of choice is SI, and for those studies which report in SI terms there is no translation problem. Many studies, however, report in native terms, and the translation of those native terms may well be to a non–SI system, such as English or American.

There can be subtle problems in doing so. For example, Freeman reported in pints, gallons, and bushels (1955). Most of us have transformed these measures into the SI system, although Hanks used pounds and tons (1972). Up to now everybody has apparently missed the fact that *gallon* and *bushel* are polysemic, meaning one thing in the English system and another in the American system. The secondary analysts have, for the most part, been Americans and have used the American meanings of the terms. But Freeman assures me that he could not have been using American pints, gallons, and bushels (personal communication). He could only have been using imperial measures, which if they are the wet measures are close to 20 percent larger than American ones, and the dry are about 3 percent different. Whether others have done so is not clear. To reduce ambiguity it is essential that the calculations be presented on a step-by-step basis—otherwise there can be little certainty in the replication.

Cultural contamination is only slightly at issue in the measure of agricultural productivity. Area, yield, technology, and genus involved can all be measured without cultural contamination. Work, on the other hand, is not cleanly conceptualized and is therefore more vulnerable to both ambiguity and cultural contamination.

There is a natural foundation for several of these dimensions. For the human technology there are only a small number of possibilities, and there seem to be few classification problems. The major problem, again, is with work. There is a strong possibility that there is some cultural contamination in the concept of work. Clearly more care and ingenuity are needed on this dimension.

Most of the measurements can be and are made by the trained observer, some of them with calibrated devices (meter, kilogram, liter, second of time). Some fieldworkers rely on trained native informants for diaries of work (Moerman 1968a; Durrenberger 1978). Rather than personally observe everything that a given individual does for a number of days, the informant is trained in how to keep a diary, and the observer collects and discusses the entries in the diary on a frequent and regular basis and in addition may conduct spot checks. There are of course sources of error here which are hard to detect. But careful fieldworkers (such as Moerman and Durrenberger) try to build in cross-checks and look for reports which diverge from the mean in the attempt to identify the anomalous ones.

In the study of agricultural productivity there is a major problem with comparability, for different outputs are by no means comparable. If we confine our study to a single major crop (e.g., rice) then by and large the observation problems do not lie in comparability. Rather they are to be found in logistic difficulties and in measurement error on the part of the observer. The major exception is the dimension of work. This dimension is so clumsily formulated that it is quite probable that cultural contamination is having an effect. It is certainly the case that the uncertainty associated with measures of work is high.

The object that we are observing is reasonably clear. It is the crop production system (involving planting, tending, and harvesting of domesticated plants and animals) in a particular locale. Of the five necessary dimensions for studying agricultural productivity, land area, technology, crop variety, and crop output are monothetic or very close to it, have unambiguous terminology, and are easily standardized. Ambiguity and cultural contamination for these four variables is reasonably low.

The exception is the dimension of work. The dimension is not monothetic, for it may include things that are not work (e.g., resting in the fields) and may exclude activities which might well be included in work (such as repairing farm equipment). It is not clear that the uniqueness rule for names applies. In addition there is the strong possibility of cultural contamination.

We tend not to see ritual as part of agricultural work, and yet ritual, both at home and in the fields, is a prominent part of many agricultural systems (e.g., Freeman's 1955 account of Iban agriculture).

Comparability in the object and in the four well-formed dimensions is achieved at a high level. This is not yet true of the dimension of work. In the case of agricultural productivity I have demonstrated that an analysis by dimension and object is feasible. Compared with phonology and ethnobiology the results are less mature, primarily due to weaknesses in the concept for work. But the strategy of analysis is productive, it has generated some results (see Hunt 2000), and some of the serious problems are on the surface, waiting to be solved.

Notes

1. Labor productivity can be thought of in two ways. In the more precise way, the productivity of the factor of labor refers to that fraction of the output that is produced by labor (as opposed to other factors, such as technology, land, water, etc.). Factor productivity is measurable, but it is very difficult to do. In most cases in anthropology the productivity that is measured is the ratio of the factor of interest (here labor) divided by total productivity. While less revealing than factor productivity, it is worth measuring.

2. Dry-foot refers to growing conditions where the soil is allowed to dry out. Wet-foot refers to soil that is continuously flooded for substantial periods of time. Rice is the only major crop plant to be grown under both conditions.

3. There are many other dimensions of the land that can be specified and measured, including slope, mix of soil particle size, pH, available N, P, K, and so forth. One of the massive triumphs of the human mind was the successful effort to disaggregate these dimensions, measure them independently, and experimentally manipulate them, starting in the nineteenth century. When outputs are matched with inputs in the context of an experiment station, very complicated and interesting analyses can be performed. For field studies it is much harder (for obvious reasons) to measure any significant number of these dimensions. But it is not impossible. As we proceed with studies of natural culture knowledge of soils, multidisciplinary studies relating the natural cultural with the scientific dimensions will become more frequent, and enormously productive. (The Behrens [1989] article on knowledge of soils is hopefully the beginning of a trend.)

4. There does not seem to be much danger of confusing a bean plant with a rice plant, or a bean seed with a rice seed. Nor do any of these get confused with mangos, or much of anything else. As Berlin has shown (1992), at least some natural plant taxonomies are elaborate and unambiguous, and they are valid when compared with scientific taxonomy. There is little reason to suspect that anyone who is paying attention is going to confuse tomato with rice, or eggplant with maize.

5. We may well have a taxonomic tree of variables (technology includes tools, which include types of energy sources, materials, etc.), and the judgment of distinctness may well need to be made at the "same" taxonomic level.

6. There are other stages of the agricultural cycle, including competitor control, harvesting, and post-harvest processing which involve different tools and different practices, but these are rarely focused upon in comparative discussions of agricultural productivity. There is no reason to leave them out, and they could easily be included in the framework. Especially if the interest is in the relationship between labor time, technology, and output, then any stage of the agricultural cycle that demands labor should be included in the investigation. As competitor control (mostly weeding) can be a major component of the labor budget, it should certainly be included.

7. Swidden, or slash and burn, agriculture is a long-fallow technique. At the start of a cycle, the vegetation (sometimes dense forest) is cut down, allowed to dry, and then burned. Immediately after the burn the crop is planted. After harvest (and perhaps not until after the second or third yearly harvest), the field is allowed to go to fallow. During fallow a succession of mostly undomesticated plants will grow on the field. When it has grown to a particular succession stage, it may well be cut, dried, burned, and planted again. The entire cycle may take as many as twenty-five years, so there may be as few as one or two crop cycles in twenty-five years.

8. Sahlins's conclusion of savage affluence is powerfully affected by the definition (or lack of it) of the dimension of work. Sahlins concluded that foragers work less than agriculturalists (1972; cf. Lee 1988). This conclusion has been widely accepted in the literature (see Kaplan 2000 for a skeptical review). Hawkes and O'Connell (1981) noted that the conclusion is based entirely on the definition of work, and specifically what is food production work. There has been some discussion of this in the literature. For example, Dobe !Kung spend some time on making and repairing hunting technology (bows, arrows, spears, bags). Hunting activity is called food production work. What are we to call hunting tool construction and repair effort? Is that food production work? And what about gathering firewood and preparing natural products for eating (peeling, cooking, butchering, etc.)? Are these activities part of food production? As is immediately obvious, the number of hours of work in "food production" is deeply dependent upon how work, and specifically food production work, are defined.

9. However, here there can be severe difficulties with native units of measure. As the discussion of measuring productivity in *Culture and Agriculture* (Schwartz 1985; Moran 1986; Loker 1988) has so clearly shown, native measures of length and area are by no means stable. Often the measure is for a day's work, and the area that a farmer expects to be covered in a day's work varies with the task—clearing, planting, weeding, and harvesting may each have different areas for a day's work. The only solution is to use scientific observation procedures if systematic comparison is intended. The natural culture categories may need to be understood, but in no case will they be sufficient. Measurement in the scientific framework is absolutely necessary. Sometimes there are no native measures of land area. Freeman (1955) reports that the Iban, for example, refused to let him measure their fields and reports no Iban measures of field size.

CHAPTER EIGHT

~

Social Organization
of Canal Irrigation

In previous chapters I have argued that we have empirical observations of
cultural phenomena that have entirely or largely achieved comparability
across cultural boundaries. Several principles discovered in the natural science section were visible in the efforts to construct empirical observation
languages for social phenomena.

The task for this chapter is to apply these principles to the subject of the
social structure of irrigation. It is an attempt to establish comparable observation procedures and is the product of a single research group. Much of what
follows has been worked out over the years (see especially Hunt 1988b).

In basic science the justification for investigating a subject is the scientific
interest and productivity of doing so. Another kind of justification for interest in a subject is practical importance. As it happens, canal irrigation has a
strong pedigree on both counts.

There is a substantial literature on the alleged importance of canal irrigation in the origins of civilization and the state. At one point it seemed as
though canal irrigation might even have a causal effect on the origin of civilization (cf. Service 1975 for a review). Associated with the names of Karl
Wittfogel (1957) and Julian Steward (1949), this position was challenged by
Robert McC. Adams (1966). Since that time much work has been done on
canal irrigation in archaeological contexts. While it may now be clear that
canal irrigation did not cause the origin of civilization, it is also very clear
that canal irrigation was intimately involved in the production of surplus and

in the increase in both minimal and mean carrying capacity of arid environments occupied by early civilizations. And many early civilizations occupied
arid or semiarid zones.[1] There is then a powerful interest in understanding
more about irrigation in the early civilizations. It was important, a great
amount of thought, labor, and materials was put into it, and a great amount
of labor organization, crop yields, and transportation was extracted from it.

In addition to the archaeological context, there are very large recent and
modern populations that are living in, and rely upon, canal irrigation systems. Their sociology and culture must at the very least be adapted to irrigation, and there may be other aspects which are profoundly important.

A major practical justification for studying contemporary canal irrigation
is that it is a critically important support for current and future food production systems. About 40 percent of the world's agricultural production depends upon irrigation (Johnson 2001). Many billions of dollars were invested
in constructing irrigation systems in the twentieth century in an attempt to
make food production increases keep pace with population increases. Almost
all of the obvious sites for building them have been taken, and there are major social and cultural obstacles to building new ones.[2]

We have spent many millennia understanding and explaining the physical system that delivers water to the field, the laws that affect the movement
of water, and the growth of the plant. Our understanding of these matters is
one of the great intellectual and practical triumphs of the human spirit. Our
understanding of the organization of human action that captures and moves
the water is far less developed, and yet it is no less important for the future
success of irrigated agriculture.

In a context of rising population and few remaining sites to build irrigation systems, there is great pressure to make more effective use of the irrigation water that we capture now. Add to this context the financial distress of
governments, and we can understand the pressure to privatize government irrigation systems (Hunt 2001). In both of these cases future food production
gains are going to depend upon effective management of an increasingly
scarce resource, fresh water. The obvious response to this will have to be to
make the existing projects more efficient and effective.

A major way to increase food production is to squeeze more crop out of
each cubic meter of water. The water-using effectiveness of a system is in part
a function of the original design (which is hard to change in small incre-
ments), and in part a function of all the phenomena which come under the
rubric of management. Many of us now believe that the largest gains in effectiveness and efficiency will come from improvements in management,
which of course entails the social organization.

Understanding and steering that management effort ideally involves scientific knowledge (as well as other skills and kinds of information). Scientific knowledge of irrigation system management starts with an understanding of the social structure of canal irrigation systems.

My major purposes for doing this work, then, are to describe the social structure of canal irrigation and to formulate and test hypotheses about the relationships of dimensions, particularly any relationship between social structure and effective operation. The substantive questions that drive this effort are rooted in the attempt to describe and explain irrigation management phenomena. I am presenting a proposal for a scientific empirical observation language for the social structure of canal irrigation. I argue that it will achieve comparability.

Because we are at the beginning of such an effort the questions will seem obvious, and the answers crude, clumsy, and largely self-evident. It should be kept in mind that all empirical observations develop through time. In the sphere of irrigation operation we are groping about in the mists of early history, compared with our measures of length and phonology. But no scientific understanding of the phenomena will emerge without effort invested in creating and improving the empirical observation language. The remainder of this chapter is an attempt to construct variables for the measurement of irrigation social structure, with a particular focus on management.

Irrigation System

For our purposes we will declare that the *canal irrigation system* is the object of interest. Almost no systems cross international boundaries, so they are contained within nation-states.

Canal irrigation itself is both easy to find and hard to confuse with anything else. It everywhere involves human efforts to divert water from its normal flow pattern so that the water flows to crop plants.

There are several natural constants involved. Liquid water responds to differences in altitude with great rapidity. It is therefore easy to determine what the normal flow channels would be and to identify where it goes instead. It is also usually easy to determine where the flow actually goes and what agent is causing this change in flow. Normally there is a distinct and visible physical system (of dams, canals, gates, and dikes) which directs this flow.

The other set of constants flow from the fact that water has the same set of functions in green plants in all crop-producing zones on this earth. The water brings nutrients in solutions to plants, provides water for the fauna in the soil, and serves vital cooling, support, and gas exchange functions through the leaves.

The leaf of the green plant gets its water from the plumbing system of the plant, and the intake is in the root. The root is located in the soil, and as one might expect there are many characteristics of the soil that affect the growth of the plant. Agricultural soil is not a purely natural phenomenon (although purely natural soils obviously support plant life).

Agricultural soil has been managed, and in some cases constructed, by the activities of man. All soils are composed of small chunks of rock, various kinds of organic matter (e.g., dead roots, dead animals); huge numbers of bacteria, plants, and animals; and pockets of space between the particles. Every particle is surrounded by a thin film of water which cannot be extracted under natural conditions. In addition to that thin film of water, the spaces between the particles may be more or less filled with water, and the remainder of the space contains air. This water solution contains ions, some of which are necessary nutrients to the plants whose roots are the intake system. The air provides the oxygen supply to the roots of dry-foot crops.

The objective of irrigation is to deliver water to the root zone of the crop plant. Ideally that water is in a good soil structure, one that allows water and air to flow and roots to grow. The water contains the right nutrients in the right amount, and most of those nutrients have been supplied by the soil particles. There is enough water so that the flow into the root and out the leaf is optimal. And there is enough air in the soil so that the roots do not drown.

The point of irrigation, then, is to provide the right amount of water, carrying only the right nutrients in the right amounts, to the plant roots at the right time. Too much water is as detrimental as too little. Too much mineral is as detrimental as too little. Water that is too early may be as detrimental as water that arrives too late.

The canal irrigation system brings water from a distant source and delivers it to large numbers of plants. Therefore the timing and quantity of water delivered is the responsibility of the management of the irrigation system. It is clear that variation in the coordination between the needs of the plant and the actions of the management system might have a profound effect upon the effective use of the water.

Given the needs of plants for water and the effect of gravity on water, the purposes and facilities are rarely at issue. Their presence and their purpose are clear to all.

A clear perception of irrigation on the ground is not yet a clear picture of a single irrigation system. Some years ago Kelly correctly pointed out that "the irrigation system" seems to function as the master analytic concept, and that it was usually left undefined. He quotes one of the few statements in the previous literature, that by Canute van der Mere, which is repeated here:

An irrigation system is an arrangement by which water is conveyed from a
source to an area needing water to facilitate the production of desired crops.
(Kelly 1983:881, quoting from van der Mere, 1968: 720)

Van der Mere's description states things that are true of irrigation systems,
but it does not tell us whether there are discrete irrigation systems, and is
therefore of no use in deciding where the boundaries between such systems
are.

Ambiguity and multivocality in identifying the unit of the object con-
tribute so much uncertainty that the results are seriously weakened. One example will make this clear. In Millon's comparative study (1962), the El Sha-
bana, a tribal group in southern Iraq studied by Fernea (subsequently
published in 1970), was one case. Millon measured size of irrigation by the
number of hectares occupied by the tribe. However, Iraqi irrigation engineers
had system-wide administrative authority. Various units of the tribe received
water from the national canals and from the engineer appointed by, and
hired by, the nation. The territory covered by the national irrigation bureaucracy was vastly greater than the territory occupied by members of the tribe
(208,000 ha versus 12,000 ha).

It is immediately clear, then, that the territory occupied by members of the
tribe was not the same as the particular irrigation system administered by the
nation. No cross-system comparability is possible if two or more definitions
of the object are in use. In nomothetic studies each variable to be measured
must be measured on identically defined objects. We therefore must have a
stable way of identifying *particular* irrigation systems.

Any large-scale comparative study is forced to rely on extant literature. It
is therefore necessary that the variable be measurable from secondary sources.
Ideally, the unit should be defined so that it is also applicable to archaeological and historical sources. What follows, then, is an attempt to specify how
to find the boundaries of particular irrigation systems.

A canal irrigation system is composed of (1) a facility (gate, offtake)
which takes water from a natural channel and guides that water away from
its natural downhill course, and (2) the subsequent control works (canals,
gates, fields) that guide the water flowing on the surface to the agricultural
plants until that water either soaks into the earth or flows on the surface out
of the control works.[3]

The objective of this chapter is to present a scientific language for observing the social organization of irrigation systems. As an example I will use
a particular substantive question: What is the relationship between the size
of the system and the system of authority? Other questions would do as well,

but this particular question is one on which there is a considerable literature, and it is important for both theoretical and pragmatic reasons.[4]

The sections that follow will display the variables that were generated to test that proposition. The object, a canal irrigation system, has already been defined. It remains to discuss the variables of size of system and charter of authority of the system. Prior to defining charter of authority, however, two other dimensions must be discussed: task and role. Most students of the subject have approached it by means of the tasks that are performed by those who manage and use the system. The reasoning for this is that management includes the distribution of the water and the performance of maintenance, both necessary to keeping the system going. The tasks are performed by roles. Fundamental to the measurement of charter of authority, then, are the specifications of the tasks to be performed and the roles which perform those tasks.

Tasks

Each and every[5] canal irrigation system presents several different tasks. They must be constructed. The water must be captured from natural flows. The water, once captured, must be allocated. Maintenance must be performed if the facility is to remain in use for more than a short time period. For all facilities with more than a handful of users, there are sets of obligations and rights which pertain to each user, and these are accounted. And finally, all systems have at least the potential to generate conflict, so conflict resolution is also a universal task, at least in theory. Two other tasks are not universally found: drainage and ritual.[6]

Construction
Some of these tasks are grounded on natural facts. The irrigation facility does not exist in nature—it must be built, for it is running counter to the normal tendency of the water flow. At the very least a trough must be dug from the natural channel across the slope. Systems vary in complexity and size, of course, so we can add longer canals, branch canals, gates which can be open or shut, cross-regulators and drop structures in the canals, escape weirs which allow surplus water to disperse without doing harm to the physical system, a diversion structure in the natural stream, and even a storage dam. As the size and complexity grow, so do the demands on engineering skill (implying understanding of the behavior of water, and materials, and their interaction) and management skill. To successfully build such a system requires the collection and coordination of expertise, labor, and materials. Large projects are justly celebrated as major human accomplishments.

Maintenance

Once the canal is built, entropy acts on the facility at all times, and so main-tenance to counter that entropy is a task of every irrigation system ever in-vestigated. There are several natural conditions which lead to the need for maintenance. Flowing water in the system has a great deal of inertia, and yet the canals in the system frequently change the direction of that flow. Canals bend around slopes, the gates often come off at right angles, and there can be steep drops in level. All such changes put pressure on the integrity of this an-thropogenic system. The pressure can easily result in breaks in the system, and then water may escape, causing two problems: a surplus of water where it is not wanted (the water that escapes floods roads, fields, houses, etc.) and a scarcity of water where it is wanted (because the escaping water is needed for plants and animals downstream in the system).

Another natural force which gives cause for maintenance is the ability of flowing water to carry solid matter. The faster a stream is flowing the larger the particle which can remain in suspension. All irrigation systems have varying water flow rates. The closer to the field gate, the slower the water flow, for the most part (channels are smaller, and volume is less). As the wa-ter slows down the larger particles settle out, and of course they settle out in the canals. As silting takes place the profile of the canal bed changes, getting smaller in cross-section and higher in bed level. The inevitable effect of this deposition is that less water will be able to flow in the channel. The conse-quence of this fact is that those downstream of the silting will not be able to get as much water. Removal of this unwanted matter is therefore another prime component of the maintenance task.

As we have seen, water is a crucial aspect of the growth of green plants. If the irrigation system has any ditches dug in dirt (as the vast majority do), the dirt on the canal banks is well watered and often has the best water supply of any soil in the vicinity. Plant life will therefore be vigorous in the canal bed and on the canal banks. The plants have several deleterious effects. They use and transpire a great deal of water (and nutrients) that might more usefully be used on crops in fields. Plants growing in the canals slow down water flow, thereby increasing siltation, thereby causing a diminution in water supply to those downstream on the channel. One partial solution to this problem is to grow economically useful plants along (but not in) the canals. In Mexico and India species of cane used for making baskets and mats are grown along canal banks and are harvested.

A frequent corollary of this plant growth is a high level of animal popula-tion. There are at least two unhappy consequences of this fact. The animals frequently build burrows in the canal banks, and these burrows can cost at least 25 percent loss in water in the canal, and at their worst they can be a major cause of weakening and breaking of the canal bank. Also the animals, which include rats, can be major competitors for the crop plants. A major chore for maintenance, then, is to clear the "weeds" from the channels and banks.

Many older systems are said to need rehabilitation. If the maintenance is not done sufficiently well, then the landscape will gradually revert to a more natural condition. The channels will fill up with solid material (water- and/or wind-borne), they will carry less and less water, and the original "natural" routes will increasingly be chosen by the water. As this process works itself out fields will gradually be denied water, and a given field will have to be changed from heavy irrigation, to light irrigation, to occasional irrigation, to no irrigation at all. Production levels will fall, and eventually the field may have to be abandoned.

A major response to this process, on the part of both national irrigation agencies and international aid agencies, is what is frequently called rehabilitation. A massive investment will be made to restore the physical system to its original design. Is this construction, or is it massive maintenance? In this case the distinction between the two may be hard or impossible to make in specific situations.[7]

Distribution
The water flow in nature has inertia, so capturing it is a human act. Similarly, the natural tendency of the water once in the facility is to take the shortest route downhill. Distribution is the process of dividing the flow and sending it to multiple users. If there are multiple sets of users, and if at any time not all users can take water from the system simultaneously, then some arrangement for distributing the water must be made. Furthermore, if a flood comes a decision must be made about how to protect it from the flood. All of this is the distribution task.

Accounting and conflict resolution are not founded in this set of geophysical factors, but rather on a different set, having to do with roles in societies.

Allocation
Simply put, there are rights to water, and the rights are allocated.

Accounting
There is water to be allocated and distributed, and there is work to be done, and therefore there are many people who are supposed to be doing the work. Often there is money owed, collected, and spent. There are buildings, paths, and other assets to be acquired, kept track of, and maintained. Accounting is

the task of knowing who has what rights, who owes what, who is owed what, and who has paid it. It can be done by memory alone, and it need not require a specialist. And one can rely on all neighbors to have a pretty clear idea about their own, and one's own, balance. A system accounting keeps track of all of it simultaneously and provides the factual solution to disagreements.

Conflict Resolution

Competition for resources is common within groups. It may occur between members at the same level of power or prestige or wealth, or it may occur between members at different levels. Two major types of activity are frequent causes of conflict within irrigation facilities: theft of water and free riding. The rules set up by a manager parcel out water to users. If some user wants more water than he is getting, he may choose to appropriate some water to which he is not entitled. This may be called theft, and it certainly can generate conflict with others.

The other form of competition is free riding. If rights are balanced by obligations (duties), then to the extent that a user can slight his performance of obligations without diminishing his flow of benefits, that individual is free riding. Since the duties associated with canal irrigation facilities can be onerous, free riding is at least as frequent a problem as water theft.

Theft and free riding may become conflicts. The existence of a conflict requires more than an act of theft or free riding, as determined by an "objective" observer. For an act to be included in a conflict, there needs to be some public statement, bringing the act into public view and usually calling into operation the conflict-management procedures and roles. For example, if water turns are measured in hours, the taking of an extra few minutes of water may not be used as a signal to call a conflict into existence. The labeling of an act as conflict requires more than the existence of that act—it also requires a social process. The social process does not automatically follow the act, and sometimes the social process is started when the alleged act has *not* been committed. Taking more water than one is legitimately entitled to may be called a theft, and that theft may be an occasion to precipitate a conflict. We must be careful, then, to clearly identify who is calling an act a theft, and what the social consequences are. There are several different participants, including farmers, irrigation staff, engineers, and other consultants for aid agencies, and social scientists. Which one of them labels an act a theft makes a great deal of difference for our understanding of the meaning and consequences of such labeling. For our purposes in this book a conflict occurs only when a dispute becomes public and engages the conflict-resolution procedures and roles.

There is of course a serious epistemological problem with this definition of conflict. It relies on the local natural culture recognizing that a conflict exists, and we are therefore dependent upon a potentially highly variable, and culturally contaminated, set of natural culture notions. In defense, it is clear that intra- and intergroup conflicts over resources are common in the animal world. There may well be a definition of conflict which can be used more or less like a phoneme—it will be efficient to use an informant to tell us that a difference in meaning occurs, but we need not rely on the natural culture to tell us what that difference means. There may, in other words, be a behavioral way to establish that the natives think a conflict exists, and we may be able to determine this by observing their behavior, not their claims.

Should theft or free riding behavior evolve into conflict, then some role may be designated as the appropriate one to deal with the problem. In irrigation facilities it is often the manager's role that has some of this responsibility, and this too is consistent with more widespread mammalian patterns.

Another source of conflict is that between irrigation systems over (usually) scarce water in the environment. In this event, the irrigation system may have rights to some of that water, it may be involved in conflict with the other system, and that conflict has to be managed.

Two other tasks are often but not universally found in irrigation systems.

Drainage
Drainage is the result of having too much water where you do not want it, and it is the reverse of irrigation. It is not universally found, but where it exists as a problem it is a very serious problem indeed. Considerable work and organization are necessary to deal with it.

Ritual
Canal irrigation systems conceived and built by international agencies in the twentieth century have no religious ritual associated with them.[8] The evidence that irrigation facilities were associated with religious ritual, and perhaps with religious temples, in the past is fragmentary but tantalizing.[9] The reasons for this are, it seems to me, obvious. Agrarian states have similar cosmologies, and water plays a critical role in that cosmology. The destructive aspects (e.g., floods, tidal waves) are often associated with evil and chaos, and the constructive aspects (e.g., rain, springs) are associated with fertility, crops, and order. There is often ritual associated with both aspects, in an attempt to control both.

～

So far then we have identified the irrigation facility as a human artifact obeying the laws of physics, and we have isolated several tasks which all must manifest or contain, based either on facts of nature or on facts of mammalian social organization.

The variable is the set of tasks inherent in a canal irrigation system. The general dimension is the kind of work to be done. That general kind is divided into several particular kinds, including construction, allocation, maintenance, accounting, conflict resolution, ritual, and drainage. All of these but the last two are universal. They are found everywhere and are anchored in the nature of the facility. The scale is nominal, and the number of scale values can be increased if need be (added to or subdivided when and if a new task is found).

Ambiguity is being reduced by careful specification of the words used to label the scale values of the variable. Uniqueness is sought. (Whether it is achieved is another matter and probably not for me to judge.) Cultural contamination is reduced partly because the tasks are related to universal physical problems of canal irrigation systems and partly because some of the tasks are a product of universal aspects of mammalian social organization (conflict over resources and conflict management). Ritual has no such foundation that I can see.

Roles

A society implies a division of labor, and a division of labor implies roles.[10] Roles are a named social position, a collection of rights and duties, are linked to tasks, and include a set of recruitment, maintenance, and termination rules.[11] All social mammal societies contain roles. Irrigation facilities of any size (greater than 20 hectares and more than ten users) have several roles, including leader, worker, and user. The tasks discussed in the previous section state that there is work to be done, and some agent has to do it. The generalizable aspects of the agent constitute a recognizable social role. These roles are everywhere (so far as I am aware) named in the local culture.

Leader
It is the case among social mammals that organized action by an aggregate of conspecifics is often organized or directed by some role that we often call "leader" in English. The vast majority of irrigation facilities do in fact have a primary leader, a person who directs water capture, allocation, and maintenance, does the accounting, and usually handles at least some of the conflict resolution. We are suggesting that this role/office be called chief administrative

officer (CAO) (Hunt, Guillet, Abbott, Bayman, et al. 2005). By no means do all facilities have a CAO, so having one is not a universal feature of irrigation systems. But the number so far found to be lacking one is about ten, while the number of systems currently known to have a CAO is no less than twenty thousand, and probably far more.

Staff

Many systems are large enough so that the CAO cannot personally perform all of the management duties, and in that case there will be subordinate staff, who are delegated by the CAO to make certain decisions and carry out certain actions. If those actions require work (as in clearing silt out of a canal) it may be done by a worker.

User

The point of the irrigation facility is to deliver water to crop plants, and these crops are grown by some human agency. That agency is usually called the user or the farmer. The issue here is who has the responsibility for applying water to the root zone of the plant. The answer is complicated by various tenure rules. The land in which the plant is growing can have several parties with simultaneous interests, including the owner, the mortgagee, a tenant or sharecropper, and someone hired by one or more of the others to actually do the work. The owner of the land may not be a natural person, but a temple, a voluntary association, or a bank. Two or more parties can have an interest in the plant itself, including the owner of the land, the mortgager, the mortgagee, and the tenant or sharecropper. Usually one of these parties has the duty to see to it that water is applied to the root zone. In most canal irrigation systems the water is delivered by the system staff to a human, not to the field or plant, although this is not necessarily the case. Wade, for example, has described a case in India where the village water guards deliver water to the rice fields, rather than to the farmers who are growing the rice (Wade 1988).

User is the name most used for that person who has (and may delegate) responsibility for receiving water from the system (from the CAO and his staff) and applying it to the root zone of the plants. User usually implies a property interest in the plants being irrigated. This is a question that needs to be answered with fieldwork, given the complexity of tenure arrangements (see Jha 2001 for an extensive discussion).

All of these roles have names in the local natural culture. All of them have criteria for recruitment, and for termination, of the personnel. There may or may not be full-time specialists occupying these roles.

The dimension being observed here is that of the roles associated with the tasks. There are social positions built deeply into the mammalian biogram (cf. Count 1973 for a discussion), so there should be no problem with finding them across cultural boundaries. The content will differ of course, but due to the task structure the basic kinds of roles will exist virtually everywhere. The scale is nominal. The lexicon can be used unambiguously.

Variable—Charter of Authority

We come at last to a discussion of the structure of power, centralization, and the like. The previous discussion of tasks, and roles associated with tasks, was necessary so that we could specify the locus of authority.

All the theories about centralization of control, or lack of it, are referring to the organization of power. In the long run we would like to have answers to several fundamental questions about power in the context of irrigation: Who has power over water, and how and why? Do those who have power over water have power over anything else, and how does it work? Do those who have other sources of power have power over water decisions, and how does that work? Finally, is there directionality between power over water, and power over anything else?

But power has been notoriously difficult to define, observe, and measure, especially from secondary literature. Since power is problematic to measure, and its measurement is all but impossible from existing sources, we turn to authority. A nearly universal context of power, especially in states, is authority—the legitimate right to wield power. Authority is rarely irrelevant to power, and at times probably maps it rather well. Authority can be observed relatively easily (compared with power) both in the field and in the secondary literature. For the rest of this chapter the emphasis will be on the structure of authority. The specific realm of this authority is the administration of canal irrigation systems.

The phrase "centralized authority" appears repeatedly in the long history of discussions of canal irrigation, and yet it is rarely defined clearly or used consistently. Kelly began the task of segmenting a muddled area into separate dimensions (1983). He noted that there are two major ideas involved in previous discussions of centralized authority: the internal configuration of authority among roles of a system and the external relationship of these irrigation roles to roles in other social systems, especially the political system of the state. Kelly wants the terms "centralization/decentralization" to designate the dimension of internal organization: ". . . the degree to which irrigation roles are hierarchically configured and authority in irrigation task performance is concentrated" (Kelly, 1983:883). He suggests "articulation/ autonomy" as a name for the degree to which the irrigation organization is linked to, or is independent of, the state.

The separation of the concept of centralized authority into these two dimensions is useful. But since the natural language term "centralized" refers to both dimensions, it is confusing to take a term applicable to an overarching semantic space and apply it to only one of the subspaces. The ambiguity inherent in natural language is very hard to avoid in this case. One strategy for solving this ambiguity is to use "centralized" for both and modify it for the two subcategories. "Internal" and "external" might be used (internal centralization to refer to the organization of authority within the irrigation system, and external centralization to refer to the articulation of the irrigation system with other systems of authority).

As a simple first question, we may ask whether canal irrigation systems have an authority system. A system without constituted authority would have a maximum of dispersed as opposed to concentrated authority and might be labeled "acephalous." A system with a constituted authority system might be labeled "unified." This is a dimension of "presence or absence of constituted authority." It has a nominal scale. We may later find an ordinal scale will be justified. The nomothetic proposition we are investigating states in effect that all canal irrigation systems are unified.

Turning to external authority, all canal irrigation systems in modern states are articulated in some way with the state. The most independent of irrigation communities often have some sort of legal permission to organize and are often jural persons (Hunt 1988b).[12] "Articulated/autonomous" for naming external relations is therefore problematic. A study of the dimensions in which an irrigation system is autonomous and articulated would be of considerable interest.

The meaning of "centralized authority" most prominent in the literature concerns the kind of linkage between the authority roles of an irrigation system and external entities, usually the state.[13] This is at the core of Wittfogel's theory and is the concept of "centralized" that Millon used in his comparative study (1962). It is the dimension that Kelly wants to name "articulated/autonomous," and it is the one in focus in this study. One way to approach the issue is to ask whether authority over the decisions and activities within the irrigation system comes from within the irrigation system or from a source external to it.

A feature of authority systems is a charter for that authority. All formally constituted canal irrigation administrative systems have some sort of charter for the authority to do the work to run the system. An administrative structure must contain work to be done and roles filled by individuals to do the work. In the administration of canal irrigation these are tasks and roles.

Several universally found work tasks have been identified, and there are roles assigned to perform these tasks. If there is a single authority structure responsible for these tasks (if the system is unified), then there must be at least one administrative role. Systems with constituted authority are headed by a CAO,[14] defined as that office (role) responsible for allocation at the facility where the system takes water from nature. There may be various subordinate staff members who are also responsible for allocation. Some or all of the other tasks and roles may be under the authority of the CAO and may be performed by the staff. The CAO usually must report to some role or set of roles (minister of irrigation, board of directors, etc.).[15] All irrigation systems contain the role of user. For some tasks there are also large numbers of workers (maintenance and construction). These workers may be full-time employees of the system; they may be farmers, part of whose responsibility is to do the work; or they may be laborers hired temporarily for the task at hand.

In 1988 I identified five kinds of charter of authority (Hunt 1988b):

(1) National government charter: The center of the polity (a ministry, or an official connected directly to the head of state) has direct responsibility for operating the system, appoints the CAO, and is responsible for formulating the rules for operating the system. In this case the authority springs directly from the center of state.[16] This is the classic top-down form of management. This is what most authors seem to mean by "centralized."

(2) Provincial government: The next form of charter is more problematic. In the vast majority of centralized management structures, the source of the charter is the national government. In India (and perhaps elsewhere) it is the government of the provincial[17] level which supplies the charter. In other respects management structures are like the nationally centralized ones.

(3) Irrigation community: These are the systems often called indigenous, traditional, or community (Beardsley 1963; Coward 1976, 1979, 1980; Maass and Anderson 1978). In these cases, there is a corporate group whose members have legal rights to the water involved, there is some irrigation-related common property which is owned and managed by the group, and this corporate group provides the charter for the authority of the CAO (Hunt 1988b, 2006). This officer has direct responsibility for the operation of the headgate.[18] The standards and sanctions for executing the duties of the office are determined and carried out locally by the

corporate group. Rules for operating the system are set by the corporate group, and formal sanctions of the staff and of members are also under the control of that corporate group. This is the classic participant-management, bottom-up, or farmer-run system.

(4) Consortium of irrigation communities: In these cases two or more irrigation communities combine to jointly manage some of their affairs. Technically, then, these consortia are not irrigation *systems* in the sense used in this book. They are groups of irrigation systems. The individual irrigation communities retain sovereignty over their internal affairs, but relationships between them are managed by the consortium. The consortium will also manage relationships with the external world (in particular the national government). In this context the major point is that these are run by farmers, not by the national government.

(5) Private: In these cases an irrigation system is run by an individual who in effect charters himself. A common way for this to occur is when an entrepreneur provides funds for the building of the system. Most of the cases known to me come from relatively highly capitalized agricultural enterprises in Latin America (particularly sugar mills) (cf. Barkin and King 1970; Ronfeldt 1973). These individual entrepreneurs come from a wide variety of backgrounds and can be merchants, locally generated "caciques" (political bosses), or foreign capitalists. The irrigation systems are seen as belonging to, in almost every sense, the entrepreneur, rather than to the nation (as in the national government chartered systems) or to the group of farmers (as in the case of irrigation community chartered systems) (Hunt 1988b). I know of a few cases from Mexico, the Philippines, and Japan but have found no more than ten of them.

With further work it has become clear that there are additional distinctions to be made (Hunt 2006). There are some supranational charters of authority, often found in colonial situations. My original value of irrigation community was challenged by Wang in his dissertation (1997). He rightly perceived that in California we had two distinct forms of organization for irrigation systems, the mutual company and the irrigation district, thereby splitting my value of irrigation community into two distinct concepts.

Communal has at least two general meanings, both referring to forms of social organization. The term is used to refer to local territorial units (such as a village, or Leiden, or Cambridge). It is also used to refer to an organization of people who share some characteristics and organization but are not territorially based. In the irrigation context *irrigation community* has been used this latter way by many of us. It now seems to me that we have several different ways of organizing irrigation systems that have been referred to as communal.

In my original meaning of *irrigation community* I included a corporate group of users of the irrigation water, who chartered their CAO. These groups exist in large numbers and are, I suggest, organized as common property resource managers (see Hunt 1986; Ostrom 1990).

There is another kind of local organization of irrigation wherein the municipality contains (entirely, or largely) the physical irrigation system, and it is the political structure of the municipality that provides the charter of authority, and perhaps even the officers, of the irrigation system. Resources for some or all of the irrigation system tasks may come from the municipality. Note that in this case only some of the residents (citizens) of the municipality are irrigators, and some nonresidents may well be irrigators as well. The irrigators may or may not dominate irrigation affairs or municipal affairs.

There is a third kind of local organization of irrigation wherein a special-purpose governmental entity is created. We have found these in California. The province provides the template for these, and they are spatially rather than hydraulically defined. A block of territory is marked out, which may or may not be isomorphic with the boundaries of counties or municipalities but are always totally within the boundary of the province. The province authorizes an election to determine whether an irrigation district should be formed. Those resident within the territory vote in an election. If the irrigation district is approved, then a special-purpose government entity is created with a bureaucracy to run the irrigation system. This entity has taxing power and the power of eminent domain. The number of farmers (or, alternatively, of owners of irrigated land) may be a tiny fraction of the voting population of the territory (see Maass and Anderson 1978; Wang 1997).

We have, then, three different forms of communal organization of irrigation (so far!). In the subsequent discussion of what we know about communal irrigation it will be useful to distinguish between these three forms. They need to be named unambiguously. I suggest that *irrigation community* has a core meaning, which is that the holders of water rights, and only the holders of water rights, are organized to manage their own affairs. I suggest *municipal* for the second type. I suggest *single-purpose district* for the third type.

The question of whether a system has a constituted authority can be answered in the same terms. A system without an authority system has no CAO. Systems can be unified (an authority system, with a CAO, is present) or acephalous (no authority system, and no CAO). (It may also be true that a system without a CAO has no charter of authority.) The scale is nominal.

Charter refers to the source of authority of the chief administrative officer, who presides at the head facility. That role is responsible for carrying out allocation decisions at that facility. The scale of the variable is nominal. The values so far isolated are international, national government (with two subtypes—national and provincial), irrigation community (with three subtypes—users, municipal, and district), consortium of irrigation communities, and private.

Irrigation systems with a national or provincial charter of authority are politically centralized. Systems with an irrigation community charter, a consortium charter, or a private charter are clearly not politically centralized, however they may be articulated with outside institutions (Hunt 1988b). The scale is nominal.

Variable—Size of Irrigation System

Three different aspects of the size of a system are found in the literature. The population of a system has been used by Millon (1962) and by Earle (1978). The length of the main canal and the total length of the canals have been proposed (by Kappel 1974). Finally, the areal extent of the system has been used by Millon (1962), Earle (1978), and Hunt (1988b). In addition, distinctions such as technological complexity have been attractive to some, and organizational complexity to others (cf. Netting 1974; Spooner 1974; Uphoff 1986). The literature is silent, however, on where and how one is to observe these features.

Use of the population of a canal irrigation system as a measure of its size is an attractive concept for many reasons. But the difficulties in conceptualizing and measuring it are very great and have not been overcome. A primary obstacle is the definition of who is to be counted in. If one focuses on the farmers, then one has to decide whether one means the landowners, the farm operators (they are often not one and the same), or the farm workers (again they may be different, partially or totally, from the two previous categories). There is the added complication that some canal irrigation systems contain, wholly within their boundaries, rather large towns (and perhaps cities), few of whose residents are connected directly to the water in the irrigation canals (e.g., Valencia in Spain, Fresno in California). Census tracts virtually never are drawn in terms of hydrological features and therefore do not differentiate between irrigators and nonirrigators. The size of the population will respond to technology, to the price of land, and to such forces as land reform and the relative strength of industrial and other sources of employment. All of these difficulties might be resolved, given the time and resources. At present, the population of an irrigation system is neither a clear concept nor can it be measured from the secondary literature.

The length of the main canal and the total length of the canals of the system would be very instructive measures to have. At the very least a ratio of extent to length of canal would tell something about the likely maintenance burden.[19] It is not clear to me that the length of the canal system will correlate with variation in administrative structure, although it might. But the length of the canal systems is only very rarely reported in the secondary literature, and therefore the concept, however interesting, cannot be used as a variable at this point in time.

Overall extent has been the usual meaning of size of a canal irrigation system. Most apparently mean the extent of the fields irrigated in the system, measured in acres or hectares. An advantage of this concept is that many authors (or government documents) publish a figure on the extent of a system. Extent is thus both useful and feasible, although it is not the only useful one imaginable.

Nevertheless there are difficulties with published figures of the extent of a given system. There are motivations to inflate the stated size by those who are responsible for the system, particularly if the system is a national government one. Often a system is designed for a given size but never actually reaches that size. Yet the designed size will continue to be the officially reported size of that system. In some systems the amount of land that is irrigated in any given year is a function of the amount of water in storage. This is true of the 53-hectare system in Pul Eliya (Leach 1961a) and of a 100,000-hectare system in northwest Mexico (Hunt 1982 field notes). What then are we to define as the size of the system—the largest number of hectares that have ever been irrigated in that system, the average number of hectares, the designed number of hectares, or the number of hectares under irrigation this season? Arguments can be mounted for each of these. It is tempting to select the average number for at least a decade as representing the administratively relevant number. I would put least emphasis on the designed size, for this is on occasion a wildly inflated number. For working in the secondary literature the question is moot, for virtually no one identifies the source of the number, much less how that number is defined.

Even more useful would be a ratio of the number of canal gates to the extent of the whole system. This would be a telling figure, for it would identify the number of decision points in the system (each gate must be operated—and the more gate operations the more decisions taken) and could very well serve as an index of administrative density.

The definition of the size of the system must be linked to the definition of the system itself. If we are to attempt to correlate two or more variables, those variables must be measured on the same basic sampling unit or object, in this case an irrigation system. The system was defined in terms of a head facility and the control structures leading the water away from the natural drainage system. The charter of authority is defined in terms of the role responsible for that facility. Size of the system, in turn, is the extent of the fields which are irrigated from that head facility. In this way, any attempt to correlate the dimensions of size and charter of authority can be assured that each measure was taken on the same object. By this means ambiguity in the meaning of the terms is reduced.

The size of the system is the extent of fields irrigated from the headgate, measured in hectares. It has a ratio scale.

It is very difficult to know how to relate extent to the casual uses of terms such as "large," "extensive," and "huge" that are often found in the literature. One important job for the future will be to calibrate the intuitive judgments about size to an explicit measure of size such as "extent" (Hunt 1988b).

The goal of this chapter is to present an observation language for the social structure of irrigation, following the principles from other analytic empirical observation languages. These results are of course rather crude, and there are many problems to be worked out in the future, and no doubt many surprises as well. There are undoubtedly some lexical items used in the measurement effort that will turn out to be ambiguous. There are surely some concepts that will turn out to be contaminated by some natural culture.

At the same time it should be clear that many problems have been identified and dealt with. Political centralization was a major problem, full of ambiguity and moral judgment. The concept of political centralization in use here is far clearer and has far less ambiguity and cultural contamination. It is therefore far more useful in comparison.

Another arena for problems is in the dividing of dimensions. The boundary between construction, maintenance, and rehabilitation of canal irrigation systems is not at all clear, and this needs further work. I have defined the system in physical terms, not in social terms. It is not clear to me what the consequences of this decision are, and there must be consequences, some of them not benign.

A point I have made several times in this book is that observation languages are never static, never finished. They evolve, as our understanding of the universe evolves, and as our measurement technology evolves. The same must be true here. It is clearly the case that our understanding of canal irrigation has progressed enormously since the 1940s, when the subject entered anthropology. Hopefully it will continue to develop. At the same time, our observation concepts and language have also evolved and should continue to evolve as long as there is any interest in the phenomenon. In this regard canal irrigation will be no different than other subjects of interest, such as kinship or weak and strong forces.

In sum, I have proposed a definition of an object, a canal irrigation system, which is anchored in nature. I have proposed a number of dimensions for observing various attributes of canal irrigation systems. They are all closer to being monothetic than before, and I have proposed a vocabulary for discussing them. The first step in exorcising ambiguity is for me to use them with single meanings. I hope to have accomplished that, but I may not have. Only further work will tell. Most of these dimensions have some sort of natural constant reference. I contend that we are much closer to having unique names than we were before. And I have proceeded by consciously using the criteria for a scientific empirical observation language that have appeared in the course of this study.

Notes

1. This includes Egypt, Mesopotamia, Indus Valley, and the coast of Peru. In many other zones water control, often through canal irrigation, was used to increase the minimal carrying capacity. Supplementary irrigation is of great use to bring a crop to harvest in occasionally marginal climatic conditions and is now widespread in the world. I assume that it was widespread in the past as well. Irrigation is widely distributed in Mesoamerica, often in contexts where the carrying capacity is substantially increased by its presence (see Doolittle 1990).

2. Obstacles include the problem of relocating those who would be flooded out, the loss of good soil to the reservoirs, a general animus against large development projects, a disinclination to interfere in nature, a desire to maintain genetic diversity, and a sense that those who must be relocated have rights to their territory. All of these factors can be seen in the reactions to the Narmada project in India but can be replicated in virtually every country. New major projects are much more expensive than the old ones in financial terms, they are much more difficult (the sites are more isolated and more marginal), and they are proving to be much more expensive in transactions costs as well, due to the social and cultural objections.

3. There are some potential problems with this definition (see discussion by Palerm-Viquera 2001). Some systems have more than one headgate, including the 12-Go in Japan (Beardsley, Hall, and Ward 1959). How this situation would affect the definition is unknown. Another potential problem is that such systems should have very clear boundaries from each other. In some parts of the world the systems are isolated from one another and the issue does not arise. However, in many other parts of the world large areas of irrigated land are covered by many irrigation systems.

The irrigated coast of Valencia, for example, has 120 continuous kilometers of irrigation, with many small named irrigation systems covering the territory. A question of interest is whether what happens at the boundaries of these systems challenges the definition of a system presented here.

4. Many analysts have beliefs about the matter, the most prominent being that large systems demand or need centralized management. Wittfogel even made a general evolutionary principle out of this, extending the effects to all aspects of Oriental Despotism. This question now has an empirical answer (cf. Hunt 1988b).

5. I do mean, at this point, that *all* canal irrigation systems manifest or contain these tasks. It is meant to be universal. If it is in fact universal, then the concepts can be applied to every newly studied irrigation system. And if the tasks are well constructed, comparability will exist as well.

6. Several authors writing on irrigation social organization have dealt with some version of these tasks, including Millon (1962), Coward (1976, 1979, 1980), Uphoff (1986), Kelly (1986), Hunt (1988b) and Jha (2001, 2002, 2004).

7. I can see no clear solution to the problem, and this problem signals a difficulty in the model. It is perhaps the case that the best dimension is one of altering nature, and it is a continuous variable. At one end there is new construction. At the other end there is regular and minor maintenance work. Someplace in the middle maintenance fades into rehabilitation, and towards the construction end rehabilitation fades into construction. It may be a single dimension, in other words, with several kinds of activity to be taken into account.

8. There is a great deal of secular ritual, performed by political leaders (and on occasion engineers) to celebrate the existence of the system and to demonstrate to the "people" the efficacy and legitimacy of the state. A significant part of irrigation engineering congresses is the pilgrimage to the headworks, usually large structures built of concrete in remote areas, and to the headquarters of the system. There will also be a ritual visit to a machine, usually a pump.

9. Bali is the major contemporary example where substantial ritual duties are embedded at every level of the indigenous irrigation system (Lansing 1991; Jha 2001). There is evidence from Peru (cf. Guillet 1992; Gelles 1992) as well. There may well be many others, but the interests and style of reporting on contemporary irrigation systems tend to ignore ritual and religion. It is impossible to know, from the literature, whether the absence of reports signifies absence in the society studied, or only absence in the report.

10. There has been a vigorous debate on what we might mean by status and role, a debate which shows the ambiguity in some of our major technical terms. The discussion in social science started, apparently, with Linton's passage in *The Study of Man* (1936), was a subject of considerable interest in the 1950s and 1960s, and has claimed less attention since about 1972. The student of social organization will note that from Linton on many have used the word *status* for the position in society, and *role* to refer to how an occupant of a status behaves in terms of rights, duties, and other things. However, in spite of this technical effort, many people continue to use

role as a term for a position in a social system, implying rights, duties, occupants, and behavior. *Status* continues to have its natural English meaning of hierarchy (Banton 1965). The technical discussions seem to have had little impact on the general senses of the terms.

I am taking a rather simple-minded approach to the problem here. I assume that social mammals operate their society with a division of labor, that the different concatenations of behaviors can usefully be called roles (i.e. I am using the more general, natural language, sense of the term), that some at least of the behavior in those roles is learned, and that some roles cannot be played by all who are eligible at the same time (e.g., there cannot be as many kings in a society as there are males). My major purpose here is to discuss comparability, and the social organization of canal irrigation, not to discuss unresolved questions in the field of social organization. Cf. Linton 1936, Bohannan 1963, Goodenough 1965, Nadel 1957, Banton 1965, Keesing 1975.

11. The roles usually have occupants, and given that social animals are alive, grow and die, there must be a constant flow of individual organisms through the roles. There are always rules for how the occupants of roles are recruited, what they do to maintain the occupancy of the role, and how their occupancy of that role is terminated. (cf. Hunt 1971 for a discussion.)

12. In an article published jointly with Eva Hunt in 1976 we argued that San Juan and Pul Eliya had centralized irrigation systems because the local elites were in control of irrigation and closely connected to the state (Hunt and Hunt 1976). I now believe that to be an error.

13. One of the meanings of "centralized authority" has been whether an administrative structure exists. This is better conceptualized as the presence or absence of constituted authority. As pointed out above, another of the meanings is that the internal administrative structure is dense, or highly organized, and so on (Kelly's dimension of centralization). This latter dimension has not been systematically studied.

14. The name for this office I originally proposed, chief executive officer, was not a good one. A better one has arisen in a collaborative effort on Hohokam irrigation (Hunt et al. 2005). We are proposing Chief Administrative Officer, which conveys that the office is concerned with execution of tasks, that it is the highest administrative office, and that it is an office.

15. There is always policy associated with unified irrigation systems. The policy-making body is often the source of the charter for the CAO. This body may have delegated some or all of the decisions to be made to some smaller subset, or it may not have. Many of the smaller "indigenous" systems make decisions based on "tradition," which is usually some policy decision made in the past and awarded nearly unchangeable status. Little is published about these policymaking bodies and about how policy is made (Valencia is an exception, where much attention has been paid to the water court [cf. Fairen Guillen 1975]). Elinor Ostrom and her colleagues (largely political scientists) have focused attention on what they call institutions, by which they

mean the rules for managing water (Ostrom 1990). Most of the attention in the literature has been paid to carrying out policy, not to how it is made.

16. In the twentieth century there seem to be many correlates. The CAO and many top-level staff have technical educations, often in engineering. The upper-level staff are paid in cash, which often comes directly from the national treasury rather than from the revenues of the system itself. Rules for operating the system are essentially set by the ministry and the staff, and formal sanctions for the staff are also under the control of the ministry. Some of the staff are urban in ambitions and culture, or want to be, and may send their families to live in urban areas.

17. An unambiguous terminology is needed for the administrative divisions of the state. I suggest that state be the unit of sovereignty, province the next lowest level, district the next lowest, county the next lowest, municipal the next lowest, followed by village as the lowest. For any given system there may be intermediate levels.

18. The CAO and other staff are often members of the corporate group, and rarely do they have technical educations. They may be active or retired farmers. The top-level staff may be paid in cash but are more likely to have no remuneration or to be remunerated with the use of land apportioned to the office or with a reduction of duties such as canal maintenance. If there is remuneration in cash it will come from the revenues of the corporate group itself. There may be no direct recompense at all. The less monetized the system, the more likely that recompense will be in relief from maintenance labor, in extra water or land connected to the office, or in produce. Such individuals are usually residents of the villages or rural towns, have a rural lifestyle, and have few significant urban aspirations for themselves.

19. It would be better to measure that maintenance burden directly, of course, and it is a major problem with studies of canal irrigation systems that the amount of maintenance work required and performed is so rarely stated.

CHAPTER NINE

⁓

Kinship and Marriage

There are several systems of terms with a universal occurrence in natural languages—plant taxonomy, animal taxonomy, color terms, and kinship terms are among them. Kinship terms, and kinship itself, have received systematic study since the middle of the nineteenth century. For a century (from 1870 to 1970) it was reasonable to expect that any cultural anthropologist knew how to observe and record kinship terms, knew how to study kinship relationships, and had a body of comparative material to provide context for the local reality. This may no longer be true.

About 1970, the focus of anthropological field studies shifted from "aboriginal" or "indigenous" cultures to the modern state and away from the traditional concepts of social structure in anthropology. It is my sense that very few of our contemporary graduate students have received systematic training in such elements as kinship, role analysis, and segmentary political systems. Around the turn of the century there seems to have been an increase in books on kinship, however (Parkin 1997; Stone 1997; Schweizer and White 1998; S. H. Gould 2000; Feinberg and Ottenheimer 2001; Scheffler 2001). Study of kinship is perhaps reviving.

Kinship and its close ally, marriage, are difficult and problematic subjects in which to achieve comparability. Although kinship has been studied by anthropologists since the middle of the nineteenth century, and there has been substantial progress made in developing an observation language, there is substantial disagreement on whether a scientific observation strategy can be effective. Leach, Needham, and Schneider, among others, have vociferously claimed that success has not been achieved. The arguments are illuminating.

Kinship and marriage have been prominent in European perceptions of "the other." It became clear very soon after contact that many "natives" had kinship and marriage customs that were significantly different from European ones. But it was assumed by most observers that what they were observing was kinship and marriage, not something else. One question that had to be faced, given all this variety, was how to describe what was being seen. It was soon clear that the usual European language terms for all these phenomena were not going to capture the details in a valid way. Some other solution had to be found.

Lewis Henry Morgan's discovery of the problem and his solutions to it comprised an early and classical case of how we work toward comparability. Trained as a lawyer and familiar with Roman law, Morgan was induced by the matrilineal Iroquois to change his perceptions of the social world. He worked out how a matrilineal society organized family, kinship, property, and political offices. He made substantial additions to our concepts for observing social structure.

A decade later, he started serious work on a comparative study of social structure (Trautman 1987:84). A major problem that Morgan (and others) set out to solve was the origin of the American Indian. Morgan thought that what we now call kinship structure would provide data to answer the question. He started his analysis by revisiting his Iroquois materials, but a field visit with some Ojibwa in Wisconsin soon convinced him that the Ojibwa were not identical to the Iroquois. He abandoned the hypothesis that all American Indian groups were matrilineal and focused instead on how American Indian kinship systems handled lineal and collateral relatives. He then proceeded to gather data from three culture areas: Europe and west Asia, North American Indians, and Asia. Most of his data from North American Indian cultures were collected in interviews, mostly on field trips. The European and west Asian data were derived from printed sources. As he suspected that the American Indians had originated in Asia, he eagerly sought data on kinship from "Asia" by persuading the Smithsonian to circulate a questionnaire to missionaries, military personnel, and others. He thought that kinship semantics was very resistant to change, and that therefore identical organization of kinship semantics in Asia and North America would indicate a common origin (see Trautman 1987 for a detailed account). Most of these assumptions have been refuted in the subsequent decades.

What is important about that project for this book was his construction of an observation language. His solution to one of the problems was a stroke of genius. Emerging from his struggles with Iroquois and Ojibwa he constructed a format for collecting information on kinship semantics. His schedule had three columns: a description of the kin type (e.g., "my father's brother"); the native word; and a translation of the name into English (Trautman 1987:99–103). Of major import is the construction of the categories in the first column. He defined these relatives in an "objective" way, by specifying a set of kin types. He would not ask for the term for "uncle," for example, but requested the terms for "father's brother," "mother's brother," "father's father's brother's son," and so forth.[1] This essentially genealogical strategy meant that he could avoid the cultural contaminations peculiar to the natural English terms (e.g., father, mother, uncle, aunt, cousin).

The results of his investigations were published with a degree of detail that is no longer fashionable, or perhaps even possible (Morgan 1871). His observation of how various kin terms refer to kin types was a giant step forward in terms of detail and specificity of reference. His work constitutes a major advance in the observation of the human use of important terms.

Morgan anchored his dimensions in natural constants, for he assumed that all societies recognized biological mothers, fathers, sons, daughters, brothers, and sisters. By designating these persons with highly specific kin types, they were named in unambiguous language. It is apparent that uniqueness was very close to being achieved. The use of the kin type specification lexicon has continued ever since. All anthropologists recognize it, and many know how to operate it. There is no authoritative institution maintaining the semantic stability. My guess is that the century of training graduate students in the arcane matters of kinship analysis accounts for the small amount of semantic change. As kinship training has been out of fashion for three decades, one consequence should be an increase in the rate of semantic drift.

Since Morgan's work in the middle of the nineteenth century, substantial progress has been made in differentiating the dimensions that apply to the domain of kinship. The kinship term system dimensions were first codified by Kroeber in 1909 and include generation, gender, lineal versus collateral, consanguine versus affine, and so on.

Marriage can be regarded as an essential component of kinship. With respect to marriage there are also a number of dimensions, such as the following: residence, gender of partners, sexuality, child-bearing, child-rearing, filiation of children, economic cooperation, and condition of partners (alive or dead). The dimensions of marriage were clarified by major efforts in the middle of the twentieth century (cf. Bender 1967 for an example).

Many of these distinctions became clearer in the dispute over the definition of marriage that centered around Gough's articles on the Nayar (Gough 1959; Leach 1961b). She claimed to have reconstructed marriage for a caste in India that was matrilineal and polyandrous. Women stayed at the family compound, while men traveled. Every woman could have several consorts and several husbands. The social father of each child was established by one man performing a ritual which connected him to that child. Thus it was clear that Nayar marriage did not necessarily entail co-residence, exclusive sexual access, male biological connection to offspring, or economic cooperation. Clearly, here was a kind of marriage that was radically different from the "normal" marriages in Europe.

What was important about this dispute from the point of view of this book is that the dimensions to be used to describe marriage were being differentiated from one another and were approaching being monothetic. As an example, it seems normal for a Euro-American to assume that a husband's sexual access to his wife, and his being the father of her child, are the same (as can be seen in Murdock 1949). Cases such as the Nayar clearly demonstrated that they are not the same and must be defined independently of each other. One must not assume that they co-occur or are in any sense the same if one is to empirically investigate their distribution and relationship. Separating the two "functions" was part of the evolution of the dimensions for observing the phenomena, thereby reducing cultural contamination in the concepts. Many such separations have taken place, and we may confidently expect that more will occur in the future.

The publication in 1970 of Ward Hunt Goodenough's *Description and Comparison*, his Lewis Henry Morgan lectures, was a landmark in a century of hard and successful work on kinship. Many of the principles of scientific measurement that are the explicit topic of *Beyond Relativism* are implicit in *Description and Comparison*. The dimensions—such as residence, filiation, sexuality, and gender—are all monothetic or close to it as a consequence of a century of close attention. The language of observation of individuals, and of relationships, now called kin types, appears to be unambiguous, and it is also assumed that linguistic procedures will validly observe the natural language terms (such as *papa*, *tío*, etc.). Much of this has been worked out since 1909 (Kroeber 1909) as part of the formal analysis (including componential analysis) of kin terms.

Goodenough attempts to remove cultural contamination from his observation procedures by anchoring his dimensions in nature. Sexual reproduction, giving birth, and infantile dependency are true of all humans, and all enduring human groups must somehow deal with them. Goodenough uses these biological universals as the foundation of kinship and marriage, and of kinship and marriage studies.

Some of the problems which remain are not connected to the empirical observation language, although they produce problems for comparability.

Goodenough bases his analysis on the human universality of sexual reproduction and infant care. One cannot object to this position. However, he takes the further step of asserting that the culture2 categories of marriage and fatherhood are also universally found in human cultures (Goodenough 1970).

It is not entirely clear why the universality of this particular folk-concept is assumed, rather than treating it as an empirical question. After all, whether a phenomenon (either the behavior, or the concept, or both) is found in a given culture depends greatly on how that phenomenon is defined. As the definitions change through time (definition of variables, and technology of observation, are in constant evolution, plus the noise of semantic drift) the perception of the spatiotemporal distribution of the phenomena may change with the changes in definition. If it has been decided a priori that every culture must have kinship, or marriage, then observation efforts are biased towards finding them. This must exert some pressure to shape scientific concepts, and thus will exert some pressure to commit errors. It is a kind of cultural contamination in our empirical observation languages.

Would it not be better if the distribution was treated as an empirical question? Would it not be as interesting to find a number of cultures (culture2 as well as culture1) without marriage as it is to assert that all human cultures have marriage?

Spiro gave a penetrating analysis of the complexities of dealing with a supposed universal concept in his 1966 discussion of the concept of "religion." In an eloquent challenge to the necessity for finding a phenomenon universally distributed, Spiro responded to an argument by Durkheim as follows:

> Even if it were the case that Theravada Buddhism contained no belief in gods or supernatural beings, from what methodological principle does it follow that religion—or, for that matter, anything else—must be universal if it is to be studied comparatively? The fact that hunting economies, unilateral descent groups, or string figures do not have a universal distribution has not prevented us from studying *them* comparatively. Does the study of religion become any the less significant or fascinating—indeed, it would be even more fascinating— if in terms of a consensual ostensive definition it were discovered that one, or seven, or sixteen societies did not possess religion? . . . In short, once we free the word "religion" from all value judgments, there is reason neither for dismay nor for elation concerning the empirical distribution of religion attendant upon our definition. With respect to Theravada Buddhism, then, what loss to science would have ensued if Durkheim had decided that, as he interpreted it, it was atheistic, and therefore not a religion? I can see only gain. First, it would have stimulated fieldwork in these apparently anomalous Buddhist societies

and, second, we would have been spared the confusion created by the consequent real and functional definitions of religion which were substituted for the
earlier substantive or structural definitions. (Spiro 1966:190)

I suggest that we have two different questions on the floor. The first is the
question of finding biological or other natural constants as the foundation for
comparative concepts. The second is the question of the empirical distribution of a cultural form or institution.

With respect to the distribution question, either the phenomenon in
question is found among all (known) human societies or it is not. Early attempts to approximate human nature relied in part on these empirical "universals" (religion, incest taboo, language, etc.). The list of these universals
has changed again and again (see Brown 1991 for a recent attempt). In this
effort a form (such as marriage or religion) is found universally, and the definition of the form is usually organized so as to conform with the known
cases. With additional evidence from new fieldwork, it is often found that
the old definition is inadequate, and new definitions have to be developed.
This is seen very clearly in the discussion of marriage (cf. Murdock 1949;
Gough 1952, 1959; Leach 1961b; Goodenough 1970). This is a very different procedure from starting from a given definition, followed by an empirical
sampling to determine what the distribution (using that definition) is in fact,
given the data and definitions of that moment.

I suggest that a major purpose underlying the assumption of the empirical
universality of an institution is a consequence of a moral strategy. One of anthropology's purposes has been to persuade civilized people that members of
relatively simpler societies were worthy humans, morally equivalent to the
members of civilizations (an example of moral relativism). It has been a long
and difficult struggle visible as early as 1549 in Spain. Part of this struggle has
been to prove that the "other" has the defining characteristics (moral as well
as biological) of humanity, including, often, religion, incest taboos, language,
and so on. It is therefore crucial, from the point of view of this strategy, to
find these institutions in every society. And so they have been. In this case,
the goal of moral persuasion has taken precedence over the goal of empirical
science. This has enhanced moral persuasion, but it has blinded us to the impact of such concerns and strategies on our empirical scientific knowledge.

The other issue is the attempt to find natural phenomena (equivalent to
the freezing temperature of water) upon which to base our dimensions. If we
can find such phenomena then we have gone a long way towards removing
cultural contamination from the dimensions we use to observe human behavior. Although this has not been enunciated as a principle before now in

anthropology (I believe that I am the first to do so), it has clearly been aimed at.[2]

Basing our concept of a cultural phenomenon on natural constants does not automatically mean that the phenomenon is universally found in human cultures. For some phenomena that is the case, as for instance in phonological analysis. But there are other phenomena that are not universally distributed (e.g., agriculture, canal irrigation). Achieving comparability in a study is greatly enhanced by finding natural constants, even though the phenomena themselves do not occur everywhere.

These two strategies have not been clearly distinguished in the past. Once they are, it can be seen that Goodenough in *Description and Comparison* has conflated the two. Conflation promotes ambiguity, and it is profitable to disentangle them.

There have been vigorous challenges to the concepts and terms used in the study of kinship, based on widespread ambiguity in our technical discussions. Needham (1971b) and Rivière (1971) in their explorations of marriage and descent come to the conclusion that neither term is sufficiently and unambiguously conceptualized to serve as appropriate analytic terms in anthropology (cf. Southwold 1971). Not only do these terms not have a single meaning, some of the various uses (claims Needham) have no meaning in common. They therefore are cases of family resemblance (following Wittgenstein—see Needham 1975).[3]

In the middle of the twentieth century the ethnographers had turned up a large variety of customs that seemed to be marriage. According to Needham these made the comparative projects impossible. One possible solution is to differentiate between the highest prestige arrangement of a mating pair, and the other forms. In rural Mexico in the 1960s, for example, there were several kinds of relationship between an adult woman and an adult man (see Hunt 1971 for an extended discussion). Casual sexual encounters were entirely possible. Another stage involved some economic transfer from the man to the woman (e.g., money, food, perhaps paying rent or buying the house for her) and/or the production of children. Another stage could be either (or both) co-residence at least part of the time and legal recognition that the man had fathered the child. Another stage is civil marriage, where the union is registered with civil authorities. The most prestigious stage is a church wedding.

One would certainly be right to conclude that Mexico, as a "society," contained the concepts, and the activities, of civil and religious weddings, both of which produced a marriage. One would certainly be right to conclude that substantial numbers of citizens did not achieve this marriage. In this Mexican case only some reproducing pairs are married, no matter what the definition of marriage used. The society has at least two varieties of marriage, but not every reproducing person is married and not every couple is married.

It seems reasonable to suggest that in the century before 1970 the respectable couples in Britain, France, Germany, and the United States were supposed to be married before having intercourse, and certainly before a child was born. The vast majority of reproducing couples at least seemed to conform to this rule. This assumption may have been operating in our thinking about marriage. If we instead adopt the Mexican point of view, then only some portion of the population is conforming to the rule, and there are stages by which one may move towards the ideal, if one chooses to. The same phenomenon is reported from the Andes as trial marriage (Bolton 1977; Custred 1977; Lambert 1977).

The Nayar may be a similar situation. They were part of Hindu Kerala, and standard marriage with a ritual is presumably found there. The Nayar (or some Nayar) had arrangements to legitimize children which varied from the standard marriage arrangements. The argument over the definition of marriage in the literature attempted to include these Nayar arrangements.

It now seems clear that the motivation was to include every person and every arrangement. It may be more useful to distinguish between high-prestige arrangements and others and to carefully consider whether "marriage" should apply to all arrangements or only to some of them. This might well reduce the ambiguity in the use of the term *marriage* and move us towards a monothetic definition that would also be useful for comparative purposes.

Needham followed Leach in suggesting a different strategy to achieve comparability. Giving up on "marriage," he asserts that the aspects of relationships (rights and duties) are comparable across cultural boundaries (1971b). Thus the "things" that exist in every culture are rights and duties, not marriage and kinship. Neither Needham nor Rivière therefore go so far as to assert the fundamental relativist position of Sapir (and later Schneider) that there are no "things" that occur in every culture. Far less work has been done on establishing the comparability of these rights and duties, so it was and is premature to conclude that cross-cultural comparability has been achieved.

The necessary solution to the problem of ambiguity in our technical language is to recognize that ambiguities still inhere in the use of our lexicon, and that therefore we have not yet achieved an unambiguous observation language. All observation languages develop, and the observation language for kinship has developed, although not as far as it might.

Does Kinship Exist as a Scientific Category?

The most sustained relativist challenge to the cross-cultural existence of things is that by David Schneider on the subject of kinship (1984). Needham challenged the scientific status of the terms *descent* and *marriage*. Schneider challenges the scientific status of kinship, arguing that the anthropological concept of kinship is only a European genealogical folk notion, falsely raised to the status of analytic concept by European anthropologists.[4] The crux of his argument is that "kinship" as a concept is profoundly contaminated by folk concepts from Europe and is in effect identical with it.[5]

Schneider was a student of Parsons, and with his book on American kinship (1968) he declared himself a cultural anthropologist in the sense of culture2. His approach to kinship thereafter was exclusively, in his eyes, in terms of the local natural folk meanings of things. Many other scholars were operating with what I am calling culture1, wherein behavior and social institutions are just as important as folk ideas. As will become clear below, this difference in approaches makes a difference. Schneider's assertions about kinship refer to a very limited set of statements about kinship.

Schneider holds that the Western view of kinship is based on natural culture propositions about human reproduction (blood is thicker than water). Schneider argues that a re-analysis of material from Yap shows that not all cultures have such views. He concludes that anthropological analyses of kinship are simply projections of a Western folk model and are distorting what is out there in other cultures. He further suggests that all four of our major categories—economy, politics, religion, and kinship—are equally suspect. This part of his argument challenges the idea that a discipline concerned with culture could be scientific. For Schneider there are only folk views. Although he often uses the term *analytic*, in effect he denies that there are (at least so far) any analytic categories, and he seemed disinclined to join the effort to construct them.

In order to confront the issue of the scientific comparability of "kinship," Schneider's position must be examined in detail.[6] Schneider's analysis of kinship is complex and contains two sets of assumptions and two different analyses of restricted empirical materials from Yap. The two sets of assumptions are (1) the doctrine of the genealogical unity of mankind, held by anthropologists, and (2) blood is thicker than water, the Euro-American natural culture assumptions about kinship.

The doctrine of the genealogical unity of mankind, according to Schneider, is composed of three assumptions held by the comparativists in anthropology.

> The first is that all human cultures have a theory of human reproduction or similar beliefs about biological relatedness, or that all human societies share certain conditions which create bonds between genetrix and child and between a breeding couple. (Schneider 1984: 119)

This first assumption is in fact two propositions. The first is that all human cultures have beliefs about reproduction. The second concerns the "bonds" between genetrix and child, and between a breeding couple. The first proposition should not be controversial. The second, found in part in the work of Goodenough and Spiro, needs to be teased apart. There are good grounds, it seems to me, to posit a material basis for a bonding between genetrix and child, based on hormones, pregnancy, giving birth, and nursing. Note that it does not assume that all mother–child dyads in fact, and all the time, manifest such a bond. Schneider means culture2, and therefore the proposition asserts that anthropologists assume that every culture2 has a theory about such a bond, not that such a bond occurs in behavior. My presumption would be that the physiological foundation of the mother–child dyad would generate bonds in behavior, that is in culture1, and not necessarily in folk theory, that is in culture2.

The last part of this proposition asserts that a bond is found, in folk theory (culture2), between breeding couples. This seems a strange requirement. First, presumably a breeding couple is not necessarily a married pair. Second, one can imagine that some (or many) couples who are breeding do so in a brief encounter. My understanding of a "bond" is that it is relatively long-lasting (more than a few minutes, or hours). I can think of no reason to assume that such a long-term bonding occurs, and find it peculiar to assert that all anthropologists assume this as part of kinship. Finally, there seems no reason to assert that this breeding couple bond would be represented in every culture2. That is surely an empirical question, and one that is likely, when addressed, to have variable results.

> The second assumption is that these genealogically defined categories, in their primary meaning, are comparable regardless of the wider context of each culture in which each is set. (Schneider 1984: 120)

The major purpose of this second assumption is to address comparability. I agree that this comparability is a central issue. The point of *Beyond Relativism* is to buttress such assumptions with a model of comparability and with detailed argumentation for why a particular assumption should be accepted. I accept that we strive for comparability. I accept that comparability is sometimes assumed. I am trying to prove that comparability is sometimes a valid assumption. Comparability for Schneider will depend upon the primary meaning of these genealogically defined categories. Presumably he is referring both to the folk concepts of reproduction and to the folk concepts concerning bonds between mother and child and between breeding couples.

> The third assumption is that differences in the specifics of different theories of reproduction . . . do not affect the fact that an abstract genealogy can be postulated which applies to all human cultures. (Schneider 1984:120)

This is again a question about comparability. Every empirical question allows for variation. The challenge is to find the constants and observe the variation validly and reliably. If one can do so, then comparability is not compromised by variation. A separate issue is the degree to which propositions in culture2 challenge comparability in culture1.

As the next step Schneider argues that the anthropological doctrine of kinship cannot be held unless the blood-is-thicker-than-water assumption is also subscribed to. The thick blood assumption emerges from Schneider's work on American kinship, is part of what he asserts is true of Western culture, and is the central part of his assertion that anthropologists have projected this assumption on to every other culture.

> Because "Blood is Thicker Than Water," kinship consists in bonds on which kinsmen can depend and which are compelling and stronger than, and take priority over, other kinds of bonds. These bonds are in principle unquestioned and unquestionable. . . . *[K]inship is a strong solidary bond that is largely innate, a quality of human nature, biologically determined.* (Schneider 1984:165–166; emphasis in original)

This proposition is about bonding, not about folk theories of reproduction. Furthermore, it is an assertion about the beliefs of anthropologists. I disagree that this assumption about bonding and kinship is held by most anthropologists who work on kinship. Goodenough (1970) and Spiro (1982), for example, derive the bonding effect from socialization, not from folk theories about reproduction. There is probably also a hormonal dimension to the bonding, which flows from pregnancy, giving birth, and nursing, although this is less well understood. However correct this "thick blood" postulate might be for Euro-American natural culture (and doubts on this matter are legitimate), it is not universally a part of the anthropological culture of the study of kinship.

Central to Schneider's claim that the anthropological study of kinship is contaminated by Western folk ideas is the claim about solidary bonding. As we will see, it is the absence of such bonding that leads him to conclude that

Yap culture2 does not have kinship. In discussing the Schneider position it is necessary to separate the phenomena of reproduction from the phenomena of solidary bonding. It is my claim that they are not linked in the way that Schneider claims, either for anthropologists or for all of the various folk that we have studied.

My view is that there are four biological constants manifest in behavior involved in human reproduction: sexual intercourse, pregnancy, giving birth, and a long period of infant dependency. There are significant differences among these constants, which in turn have different effects upon the analysis of kinship features of societies.

Mating can occur many times in the course of a human life—five thousand does not seem an outrageous number (forty years times 125 occurrences per year). But many of these matings occur in secret (there are no witnesses), many do not result in pregnancy, and no society can successfully keep track of all of them. This makes mating a poor candidate for a natural constant base of an observational category if we want to link a specific mating incident to consequences, such as pregnancy. Goodenough uses "fatherhood," a jural relationship, instead (1970).

Infant dependency is an undoubted biological and social fact. All societies appoint somebody, and in nearly all societies the biological mother, as the responsible person (reinforced by the biochemical and social implications of nursing for both parties).[7] Given high rates of death and divorce, it is clearly the case that many societies must have other arrangements as well. Every society must arrange for the care of the infant—it need not be a biological parent, although it usually is. We have then a natural constant, a feature of all human societies.

Being born is something that happens only once to each individual, and few women give birth as many as a dozen times. Apparently every woman remembers at least those births that produce a living person, and this linkage between mother and child is rarely denied or forgotten. The mother–child birth link is thus an excellent candidate for one natural constant at the core of kinship (Bohannan 1963; Lehman 1985).

Every society so far investigated has a system of kin terms (Brown 1991). The kin-term systems contain information about birth links between people. Another feature of the system is the domination of multiple cross-linking reciprocals. If you know any term, you also know its reciprocal, the implied other statuses and their terms, and their reciprocals, and so on to the limits of the system. Any person who is in such a system has all the terms to use (alter need not be alive, especially if the system has a reference function).

To take an English language example, if we start with the terms *father*, *mother*, *husband*, *wife*, *daughter*, *son*, *brother*, and *sister*, we find that in the kinship sense they form a system such that the use of one of them implies all the others. If you use the term *brother* for someone, it implies not only a reciprocal (brother or sister) but also that the two of you have a father or mother in common, and therefore you have at least one grandparent in common. If your father or mother has a daughter, she is your sister.

This system of interlocked reciprocals is extended throughout the kinship term system. If your mother has a sister, that sister is your aunt and you are her niece or nephew, her children are the nieces and nephews of your mother, and they are your cousins, and you are their cousin. Any reciprocal leads to more reciprocals. This is a dense lexical system with boundaries.

The system of kinship terms is fairly easy to find, for it usually has only twenty to thirty lexical items, always has reciprocals, is a closed system, and always contains information about birth links. These kinship terms occur in the natural language. So far it seems correct to conclude that all kin-term systems contain propositions about the biological relatedness of at least some of the roles referred to in the terminology system. As Morgan (1871), Murdock (1949), Eggan (1950), and many others have shown, there are many other phenomena which are associated with the kinship terms, including residence, incest taboos, inheritance, succession to office, and bonding (loyalty, intimacy).

Due to the dense overlap of kinship and other phenomena, there is a tendency for kinship terms to have multiple additional meanings. The natural culture term for father is often polysemic; it can be used in the kinship system, in a system of terms for statuses in the household, in the religious congregation, and elsewhere.

In sum, anthropologists have generated propositions about kinship as a scientific concept which are grounded in natural constants and which are manifest in a lexical system called kinship terminology. These do not seem to this writer to be particularly ambiguous, or to suffer from cultural contamination.

Does Yap Culture Have Kinship?

Schneider has claimed to have demonstrated that Yap culture does not have kinship in the European, genealogical sense. He also claims that his finding supports his argument about the cultural contamination of our scientific concept of kinship, and thereby challenges the past existence of a scientific empirical observation language for the phenomena of kinship.

It seems to me that there is plenty of evidence that many societies conform to the anthropological scientific ideas about kinship. The question is whether such a sense is universal or has a more limited distribution. If we are in search of a universal, then one negative case is a demonstration of the lack of universality.[8] The central empirical issue with this part of Schneider's argument is whether he has in fact demonstrated his claim about Yap. I argue that he has not done so, even in the terms he claims.

In his 1984 book, the first substantive chapters (2, 3) present two different views of "kinship" on Yap, the first a synthesis of "standard" views, and the second a re-analysis of some features of Yap social organization which challenges the first view (1984). Chapters 7 and 8 consider two sets of Yap relationships along the same lines.

The standard view as presented by Schneider focuses on two Yap institutions, the *tabinau* and the *genung*, and on two pairs of terms, *citamangen-fak* and *citiningen-fak*.

Tabinau

Tabinau refers to an estate. Centered on a sacred stone house mound, it also includes arable land, trees, fishing traps, lagoon fishing spots, offices in the extra-domestic political system, incorporeal property rights (to magic, ritual, etc.), and the headship of the estate. This is a classic Micronesian complex estate. It is normally occupied by people in "kin" relations to each other, and it is exogamous. The "head" (*citamangen*) is "married" to a woman who works on the arable land and produces children. The oldest male child will inherit the headship, and the female children will marry and move to the estates of other males. Schneider called the *tabinau* a patrilineage in his "standard" view.

Citamangen, Citiningen, and Fak[9]

The terms *citamangen* and *fak* are used to refer to every relationship on Yap that is structured in terms of hierarchy. The head (*mafen*) of the estate is *citamangen* to all others resident in the *tabinau*, and those others are *fak* to him. *Tabinau* are the units of political systems (villages, districts, etc.), each of which contains offices. The officers are *citamangen* to the numerous subordinates. In addition, Schneider says that a father and son are *citamangen* and *fak* to each other.[10]

The terms *citiningen* and *fak* apply within the *genung*, and a boy and his mother can use them to refer to each other. In addition, the *tabinau* is an environment in which the terms are appropriate, for a boy is *fak* to his mother's *citiningen* in the *tabinau*.

In his revised view the *tabinau* is re-analyzed as merely a group that occupies the estate; it is not a descent group, and in addition it is not a kinship group. Schneider presents two crucial facts here. One is that the head may select his heir and is not confined to selecting from among his children. Children are supposed to take care of elderly adults, and the oldest male is supposed to inherit the headship of the estate. In the event that a son as heir apparent does not take care of his father, disinheritance may legitimately follow. In that event the head may select "anyone" to be the heir. The dispossessed son is then no longer *fak* to the *citamangen* of the *tabinau*, and the new heir does become *fak* to the *citamangen*.

The other crucial fact is that in the event of a divorce and departure of their mother, the children stay in the *tabinau*, and must use the term *citiningen* to refer to the (new) wife of the *citamangen*, or head of the estate. They stop using the term to refer to their "real" mother.

Standard analysis of kinship always deals with kinship terminology. There are other uses and meanings of the lexical items from the kinship term system, and these are called, by some, extensions, metaphors, or other terms. Thus, part of persuasion and play (and deception) in a society can be the metaphorical use of one of the terms. But if the terms *brother* and *sister* are used for members of a revolutionary cell there is no use of the extended system of reciprocals. These metaphorical siblings do not share fathers, mothers, cousins, siblings of parents, parents of parents, and so forth, all of which is true of the kinship system use of the symbols.

I argue that in metaphorical extension the terms are not used as kinship terms. Only some of the meanings of the terms from their kinship context are being exploited, or used. Their use in this context is not a proof that genealogical kinship does not exist. Nor is it a proof that it does. The only way to prove that genealogical kinship exists is to find the system of terms/relationships. And a major way to prove that genealogical kinship does not exist is to demonstrate that the system of kinship terms does not exist.

Many of us claim that there is genealogical reference in the kinship system, and it is always a birth link. (I prefer the birth-link essential definition of kinship to the sexual intercourse link.) It may not be the only meaning, and I suspect that it is virtually never the only meaning. In every culture there are other systems of meaning loaded on to the kinship lexicon, including rights and duties connected with roles and with the dyadic relationships of roles. Furthermore there are probably, in every society, standard emotional expectations of any reciprocal relationship, and therefore these emotional expectations are also part of the semantic load of the kinship system terms and relationships.

Schneider concentrated on a very few statuses in the Yap *tabinau* household system and did not deal with that system of symbols that is called the kinship terminology, which in large part maps a genealogy. It is plausible that two of the social relationships in the *tabinau* (*citamangen-fak*, or head heir, and *citiningen-fak*) are concerned with offices in the estate as well as with roles in a kinship system. (Whatever else it is, the *tabinau* is almost certainly not a patrilineage. In 1953 Schneider reports that a married daughter is a member both of the *tabinau* of origin and of the *tabinau* of marriage [1953: 216]. This is a peculiar rule for a patrilineal descent system.)

This is possibly the case with the *tabinau* on Yap. If so, it would account for the changes in personnel in the statuses of the *tabinau*. Thus, *citamangen* may be both a kinship term and a term for an office in the estate. Schneider's published accounts (1953, 1984) make no attempt to do a systematic analysis of the whole kinship term system, and of the estate status system, or to look for the relationships between them.

Genung

The *genung*, variously called (in English) a matrilineal clan and a matri-sib (Lingenfelter 1975), is a set of people who are descended from an original ancestress and who must not have sexual intercourse with each other. There are reputed to be about thirty to forty such sets on Yap. There are subsets, called sub-sibs by Lingenfelter (1975), that can and do trace exact genealogical links with each other, and who interact.[11] Labby argues that these matri-sibs move on to a *tabinau* (1975). The marriage of a woman is an extension by her matri-sib of origin to colonize a new *tabinau*. With luck she will produce children, work hard, and her matri-sib will have taken over another estate (in the person of a son who inherits the titles, offices, etc.). In this analysis, one matri-sib inherits an estate from another matri-sib.

The central fact in this case (for Schneider's argument about kinship) is that should the woman lose or drop her membership in the *tabinau*, her children are left behind when she leaves, and those children will refer to the new wife of the head of the *tabinau* by a term they used to refer to their mother, *citiningen*. Schneider uses this fact as evidence of the lack of kinship on Yap, and it is again the bonding issue. Schneider concludes from this that the *genung* is a descent group but is not a kinship group (1984).

The *genung* presents a different set of problems than those posed by the *tabinau*. The *genung* is a set of consanguines of the uterine persuasion. Membership is determined by birth link between mother and child. The incest taboo applies to members of the genung (Lingenfelter 1975; Schneider 1984). Presumably there are a set of kinship terms labeling the various statuses in this system, this set contains the structured reciprocals discussed above, and an explicit statement of birth linkages between the members. The only analysis of the kinship term system known to me is in Schneider's 1953 article. He does not present an analysis of reciprocals, and his chart (of kin terms and kin types) on page 219 does not permit a satisfactory analysis. Schneider calls the *genung* a descent group, and the descent group by definition involves birth links between people. Schneider's assertion that the Yap do not have genealogical kinship is refuted by the *genung* if the intense bonding definition of kinship is rejected.

The crucial empirical question is what happens to *genung* membership when a person's "real" mother is no longer married to the *citamangen* and moves back "home"? This can occur due to divorce, or to the death of her husband. Full support of Schneider's argument requires a crucial set of facts. First, we must know the relationship of these children to their mother's *genung* after their mother has been displaced from the *tabinau* (Schneider's article on incest concentrates on the *tabinau*—the *genung* gets only a paragraph which has none of the necessary information [1957].) What happens to the kinship terms in such a case is important. To support Schneider's conclusion it would have to be the case that the children of the departed mother drop membership in her *genung* and become members of the new wife's *genung*. This would mean that the incest prohibition shifts from one set of people to another. Former siblings would now become sexually available, and the "new" siblings would not be available. This scenario of changing from one incest taboo group to another seems highly implausible. None of the authors considered has presented facts on these matters.[12]

Schneider's case would be made if the children became members of the *genung* of the head's new wife and lose membership in their original *genung*. So far no facts supporting this argument have come to my attention. On the other hand, if these children remain members of their mother's *genung*, and the incest regulations of that genung continue to apply, and do not apply to the new wife's *genung*, then Schneider's conclusions about the absence of kinship would be refuted.

In the *tabinau* there are positions which are supposed to be held by kin (heir, and mother), but the "real" relatives can be replaced (by whom is not stated—Schneider implies that nonkin may occupy the statuses). Thus the solidary bonding aspect of kinship which is contained in Schneider's doctrine and in the "blood is thicker than water" assumption is overridden. That overriding is apparently Schneider's reason for concluding that kinship does not exist on Yap. And it should be noted that this overriding is not confined to Yap—it occurs in Mexico (E. Hunt 1969).

I conclude that Schneider has not demonstrated that the culture of Yap does not contain kinship. All Schneider has done is show that some dyadic relationships which normally recruit consanguineal kin to one of the roles may recruit persons who do not have the normal consanguineal conditions. His case is therefore only a challenge to his definition of kinship which requires solidary bonding. It is not pertinent to a genealogical definition of kinship stripped of its bonding feature.

Culture1 vs. Culture2

If the empirical case from Yap is weak, there is still the radical relativist position, that different cultures contain different things. A logical implication of this position is that one, or some, or many cultures may not contain the dimension "kinship," or any other dimension of anthropological analysis. Schneider has a position on the goal of anthropology that is relevant to this argument.

Schneider claims that *the* aim of anthropology is the analysis of culture, and by culture he means culture2, the symbolic system of the natives (Kuper 1999).

> Anthropology, then, is the study of particular cultures. *The first task of anthropology, prerequisite to all others, is to understand and formulate the symbols and meanings and their configuration that a particular culture consists of.* (Schneider 1984:196; emphasis in original)

It is crucially important at this point that the reader keep clearly in mind the difference between the two cultures, culture1 and culture2 (as laid out in chapter 1). Culture1 is all structured behavior learned by humans as members of society. Culture2 is confined to the shared understandings, to the meanings, to the symbol system, of the members of a particular society.

At the beginning of his work on American kinship, Schneider insisted that culture2 was only part of the story (1968), and in this he was consistent with the Parsonian framework. In the 1984 book on kinship, however, Schneider had stripped his account of any mention of personality, social systems, economy, ecology, and so on. Here he is arguing in effect that culture2 is the only subject of anthropology.

In this very reduced context, it is clear why he comes to the conclusion he does about kinship. For him kinship is entirely, and only, the ideas about things held in native belief systems. There is no behavior, there is no action observable by outsiders, there is no social organization, there are only the folk concepts. (In addition, he seems to believe that analytic concepts are not possible.)

According to Schneider, the critical question is whether any particular culture contains some idea. For Schneider kinship is only what natives think. Since natural cultures have phonological systems and grammatical systems without ever thinking about them, it would be logical for him to conclude that our categories of phonology and grammar are not found in any natural culture and are not something to be dealt with in anthropology. This last statement is clearly not true if we understand "have" in the sense of "learn and use." It would be true only if we insisted that the natives have a concept of phonology or grammar. This seems to me an unproductive use of the word *have*.

There is another way to approach the subject. Suppose that some of human structured behavior is kinesthetically learned movement (including some vocal and verbal behavior). Suppose further that there are interlocking systems of such behaviors. And suppose further that there are *no* shared ideas, conscious or unconscious, about these behaviors. In this case it would be impossible to call them culture2, in the narrow restricted sense of Schneider or Sapir. In the sense of culture1, of course, they would be included.

I think it possible that many systems involving large-muscle movement—such as hunting, swimming, plowing, and sailing a boat—are learned with few or no words and can invoke few if any conscious thoughts. I would assign them to culture1 (they are learned socially, deeply structured, and last over generations). But if my thought experiment is true to some facts, then these activities would not be assigned to culture2. And if Schneider's parsimonious view of culture were to prevail, then vast amounts of interesting structured learned human behavior are not of interest to the anthropologist.

I do not understand why the Schneider view is attractive to anybody. It may be merely a matter of taste.[13]

Can we then generalize from language to kinship? Almost certainly. If we find that a (very large) number of societies possess a system of words that we can readily call a kinship term system (systematic and dense sets of reciprocals, and a proposition about the relationship between the genetrix and the child), and if we can observe and describe the attributes of the system, then we have a strong candidate for a scientific concept. We can, and always choose to, investigate what the indigenous meanings attached to the terms are. But if it is a system, and it is used to discuss birth relationships (among other activities), there seems to be no reason not to call it kinship, no reason not to say that it has a genealogical component, and no reason not to say that it is part of scientific culture. The question of the distribution of this concept of kinship in time and space is another matter entirely. It is conceivable that some human population does not have what I am here (with Scheffler and many others) calling kinship. Montague has stated that feeding, not birthing, is the crucial fact for Trobrianders (2001), and of course this claim needs to be replicated. With Spiro (1966) I regard this as extremely interesting rather than a severe blow to our understanding of culture and of human nature. The refutation of a universal distribution will have no effect on the scientific status of the definition.

Next we raise the issue of how Schneider's view of culture relates to the existence of scientific concepts. Schneider clearly has a concept of what was at the time called analytic concepts; he just contends that kinship (and probably economics, politics, and religion) is not among them. Schneider contends that the analytic concepts should apply to the analysis of his version of culture (1984). Here we must be careful. The analytic concepts about the structure of language do not apply to natural culture conceptions of language (necessarily). They apply to something quite different, the structured behavior (language use) produced in a natural culture. What the folk think about phonology and how we observe and analyze phonological behavior do not necessarily have anything to do with one another. It is similarly the case with agricultural productivity.

However interesting folk views of such matters might be (and we have no full explications of Yap or American folk views on any of these matters), my goal has been quite different. The analytic or scientific concepts have not necessarily been designed to analyze, or account for, natural culture meaning systems (culture2). They are designed to account for regularities in behavior which we as scientists can observe. With this view of the matter it is important that the analyst differentiate between a folk view of a matter and the analyst's view of a matter. This caution is probably observed more in the classroom than it is in the field or at the keyboard. There is probably a good deal of conflation of native opinion with observer perception in our ethnographic reports. Jacobson's *Reading Ethnography* (1991) cautions us to be careful about evidence for folk views and for behavior. As scientists we can also choose to account for regularities in native meaning systems, and this is precisely what the ethnobiologists have been doing with remarkable success.

Because Schneider had such a narrow view of what we should study it is not clear that there are, or could be, any scientific concepts. If the objective is to study the natural culture view, then we are limited to the content of the folk views. And given that some claim free variation in human symbol construction there is little reason to suppose that there could be *any* scientific concepts. Pushed to the extreme, then, Schneider's objection to kinship is a challenge to the existence of any scientific concepts at all for the study of culture2.

Spiro has a different view, and in my opinion a more reasoned and productive one. Spiro, another major follower of the Parsonian framework (although Spiro was trained at Northwestern and was profoundly influenced by Hallowell), has always insisted that anthropologists could not study culture alone, and further insists that the realm of culture2 is not subject to endless arbitrary difference (1984, 1986).

It is clear that the scientific status of the study of kinship is less evolved than for phonology, ethnobotany, or agricultural productivity. But at the same time there has been very substantial evolution in our concepts since the middle of the nineteenth century. Maine, Morgan, Rivers, Kroeber, Lowie, Murdock, Gough, Evans-Pritchard, Fortes, Bohannan, Needham, Goodenough, and Scheffler, among many others, have been attacking the problems of ambiguity and cultural contamination and achieving greater resolution. We still argue about ambiguity and cultural contamination, which is as it should be. We do not yet have a stable, unambiguous, and culture-free language which we can use to record our observations of kinship matters.

The principles at work in fighting ambiguity are the time-honored ones— to strive for monothetic dimensions, using the unique name rule. Given the pressures for semantic drift over time and space it is not easy to even approach success. But there can be no doubt that progress has been made over the last 130 years.

Reducing cultural contamination is also not easy. The principal strategy has been to use studies of empirical cases to bring to the surface the assumptions of the analysts. Those assumptions can often be identified as cultural contamination. One solution is to consciously choose dimensions that are located in natural constants. The favorite choices in kinship have been women giving birth to particular individuals, infantile dependency, and sexual intercourse. (The latter of course is more problematic to observe than the other two.) There is no doubt in my mind that cultural contamination has been reduced over the last 130 years. It is almost certainly not yet to zero, and the natural constants are still contentious.

The study of kinship, in other words, has an observational language that has evolved towards less ambiguity and less cultural contamination since 1871. It has achieved considerable comparability over this time period. At the same time it is still evolving, and hopefully will continue to do so. I see no reason to conclude that the effort is hopeless from the start. Nor do I think that any current state of affairs (whether 1871, 1909, 1949, 1952, 1961, 1970, or 2001) is the end point of the developments. I see reasons for being an optimist.

On the other hand the field of sociocultural anthropology is apparently very far from being ready to sit down and decide on the meaning of terms in the observation language. Firm control over the semantics of the observation language will be impossible to achieve until there is a widespread consensus that it is both possible and desirable. If history is any guide (and it usually is not), it will take at least another fifty years before the first international convention on kinship terms is held.[14]

Notes

1. The question of how accurately these natural language terms were recorded and represented by Morgan should be addressed. As long as identities are valid, it may make no difference if the representation in the Roman alphabet is phonemically accurate. Same versus different would be the crucial distinction.

2. This may be the same as attempting to construct a list of human needs (à la Malinowski) or listing a set of human biological capacities. There have been many attempts to construct such a list, presumably not based on empirical evidence but generated by theory or based on contemplation of what is held in the head of the analyst. In this category I would include Spiro's attempts to define religion and Aberle et al. (1950) on functional prerequisites of human society.

3. Sperber (1996) agrees with Needham that "marriage" is a family resemblance proposition. Sperber is using culture2 in that "marriage" is composed only of representations. There is no reason to expect culture2 approaches to be free of ambiguity.

4. The book received almost no attention in the general professional literature when it came out. I have been able to find only two reviews of the book (Damon 1986; Weiner 1988). There are no reviews in MAN, nor are any listed in *Book Review Digest*. Weiner in Oceania accepts his conclusion on Yap. Damon is more skeptical. Shimuzu (1991) has presented a critique of the book, and Schneider has responded (1992). But see now Feinberg and Ottenheimer (2001).

5. Schneider did consider that there was only one "western" view of these matters. Ottenheimer argues that there may well be several, including European and American, and that they differ (2001:120).

6. Readers who have no great interest in the details of this kinship case might want to skip to the summary of the argument.

7. There is a problem with what we mean by "society" in this case. Gough's case of the Nayar in fact concerned a rather small subcaste of one region of India. Yet her Nayar case has been treated as equivalent to the Hopi, Japanese, and others. Agrarian states have aristocracies, and among the aristocrats the women are often not the primary caretakers of their offspring, those jobs (nursing, training, watching) being assigned to others, usually but not necessarily women. It seems clear that the society as a whole has mothers raising infants, and that only a small fragment of the society (at least in population terms) delegates the job of infant care to those who are not the birth mother of the child. The issue then is the definition of the social unit— what is the boundary of the society. There has been no clear discussion of this issue in the cases of stratified societies, and it is a problem badly in need of exploration.

8. Another possibility, a "near universal" as discussed by Donald E. Brown, is a different matter (1991). Here a single negative does not demonstrate the lack of a near universal. I do not understand the purpose or the function of a concept of a "near-universal."

9. In Schneider's article on Yap kinship terms these are presented as *citimongog*, *citiningog*, and *fakag* (1953:219).

10. In his 1953 article on kinship terms Schneider states that all of his "kinship" terms are used in reference only. They are never used as terms of address (1953:219).

11. Schneider further identifies a subset, the *nik*, which can trace genealogical links to a specific ancestress. He claims that the membership in *nik* is largely secret (1984). This poses two puzzles. (1) If the incest prohibition applies to members of the set, how do two potential sexual partners find out whether they are forbidden to each other? (2) Does not the *nik* constitute kinship since it is genealogical?

12. A fuller examination of the question would involve a detailed analysis of all data on the social structure, including the kinship system, for Yap. Having read much of the material published in English, it is my sense that the crucial data are missing. In any case, a detailed re-analysis is well beyond the scope of this book.

13. This is Service's view (1985).

14. Since it seems to take about 150 to 200 years to hold those first conventions, I would not expect the first before sometime around 2030. This assumes that kinship is still a subject attracting interest and students. That is not guaranteed.

PART IV

CAN WE COMPARE
APPLES AND ORANGES?

CHAPTER TEN

~

We Can Compare
Apples and Oranges

Comparison is necessary for anthropology, and impossible. Evans-Pritchard, attribution by Rodney Needham

This book starts with the assumption that a scientific cultural anthropology is worth doing if it can be done. The problem addressed is how we might go about doing it.

I have argued that there are two major projects in anthropology, the first the effort to "get the local reality right" and the second a set of comparative questions that use the data from the local reality studies.

Getting the local reality right involves some standard activities, including engaging in thousands of hours of observation, dealing with propositions in the local natural language, and acquiring a degree of competence in surviving in that context. The literature on the subject contains both systematic instructions and personal accounts. For a good account of a lifetime of experience see Wax (1971). Bernard (2002) has written a superb manual for guidance in conducting fieldwork. For personal experiences see Bowen (L. Bohannan) (1954) and Malinowski (1967).

The "comparative" project includes several quests—synthesizing a larger entity than the local reality, synthesizing an historical trajectory, inquiring into correlations of features across local realities, and searching for human nature (however *human* is defined).

A scientific cultural anthropology is focused primarily on the comparative project and has to face squarely the question of comparability. If we cannot find comparables we have no chance of constructing a scientific cultural anthropology. A number of challenges to comparability are in the literature. The two plausible challenges are cultural contamination of concepts and ambiguity in naming those concepts.

Cultural contamination is closely linked to the natural culture origins of all of us. We are from birth trained in at least one natural culture, and it is composed of (among other things) perceptual software. It is easy for someone trained in one natural culture to use the concepts of that culture to perceive and evaluate all events everywhere. The home or native natural culture becomes the perceptual screen for seeing the world. It produces cultural contamination when it is used to look at another natural culture.

The other plausible challenge is ambiguity. If a single concept has two names, or worse, if a single name refers to two or more concepts, it is difficult to know, and keep track of, what is being talked about. The results using ambiguous names are not comparable. Natural languages are rife with ambiguity, and that ambiguity is important in poetry and politics. A science, on the other hand, must operate with a minimum of ambiguity, and is always fighting against the forces of ambiguation.

Comparability in Natural Science

The natural sciences have evolved highly successful strategies for dealing with cultural contamination and ambiguity. They have also evolved a strategy of differentiating dimensions and objects. The discussion in this book is an attempt to evaluate the utility of these strategies for a scientific cultural anthropology.

Natural science has a strong interest in the correlations of things. They ask what is associated with what and whether that association is lawful. There are two kinds of "things" (in most cases), and they are dimensions and objects.

Dimensions
Length and temperature are good examples of dimensions. They are manifest in many different objects. Dimensions are best when they are simplest—the concept includes only that dimension and is not mixed with another one. Temperature and air pressure were combined in the early thermometers, and when they were separated much progress was made in understanding both, and their correlation. Ideally a dimension is monothetic (there is only one).

The problem for science is to make sure it is the "same kind of thing" no matter where it is used. Natural cultures all have concepts of length, but some are polythetic, and few are exactly the same as those in another natural culture. One way to combat this is by military prowess—the winner establishes the standard. But any military conquest is temporary.

One effective solution is to establish a social structure whose responsibility it is to stabilize the matter. It will be multicentric and will include representatives of the major stakeholders. Let us call these a convention. Conventions call meetings at regular intervals and consciously consider the concepts which are being used as well as the names which are attached to the concepts. All conventions are empowered to change the definition of concepts or the names attached to them, and they sometimes do. The most prominent one now is the SI convention, but there are hundreds more. These conventions combat cultural contamination and ambiguity. In the most mature of them these challenges to comparability have been eliminated. The concepts (such as length, mass, and degree of temperature) are defined carefully, a name is decided upon, and the definitions are carefully translated into a number of natural languages. If possible a standard is established. If that standard is a natural constant so much the better.

The natural constant establishes comparability. It is part of the definition of the dimension. Because it is independent of any natural culture it establishes comparability. A degree of temperature (Celsius or Kelvin) is 1/100th of the difference between the two phase shifts of distilled water at one atmosphere. On this planet during the existence of *Homo* this is always the same kind of thing. Comparability has been achieved.

Objects

The "object" is the space-time place where one goes to observe dimensions. All natural cultures name many objects, and prominent among those named are organisms and human constructions (e.g., tools, pots, houses). These objects are easy to see because they have boundaries. Every science must be able to construct comparable concepts of objects. Otherwise the observation of dimensions (and their subsequent correlations) would make no sense. The same problem of comparability as with dimensions exists with objects—the same kinds of "thing" must be established, and they must be named without ambiguity.

When the "objects" have natural boundaries the problem is difficult but not impossible. Taxonomists of life forms have fixed upon type specimens which are used as standards for any organism. In difficult cases the organism at hand is compared with the type specimen to help decide if they are both the same kind of thing. Again conventions have come into being, the major ones dealing with biological organisms. Concepts are debated and defined, and names are assigned.

But there is a serious problem with "objects" that are collections, or sets, or aggregates, of things, such as communities, populations, and societies. Here there is no clear-cut boundary, and deciding what is in and what is not in is very difficult. The operational solution to this problem on the part of anthropological fieldworkers has been to focus on events in a local interaction system. Judging from the positive results of these investigations we are dealing with something real out there. But our ideas about the edges of them, and of how they combine into larger units, are perhaps far fuzzier and less reality based than we imagine. Communities, societies, and regions are not demonstrably less fantastic than ghosts and goblins. The social sciences of ecology and anthropology have a serious problem with their social objects, one that needs a great deal of sustained thought and investigation.

In addition to dimensions, objects, and conventions, there is another aspect of science that is relevant here. No observation in science is naive. All scientists have to be trained to recognize objects appropriately and to perform the observations reliably and validly. This training takes place in apprenticeships in the lab and in the field. In science, observations must be replicated to be accepted as real, and this means multiple sets of trained persons who practice what they know.

It is thus clear that science is not a natural culture. It is international, timeless, and committed to the extirpation of error. In its observational technology, it strives for, and often achieves, monothetic dimensions which are uniquely named. The objects are the product of concepts which are classical categories. The forces of cultural contamination and ambiguity are under conscious control by a set of persons. Science values finding and excising errors, whether in observations or in correlations (see D'Andrade 1995). In many cases, a social structure exists which is central to achieving these aims.

In these regards, then, science is not a natural culture and is not a part of a natural culture. It is radically different from the normal operations of natural cultures. No natural culture is systematically working to eliminate error or ambiguity. Natural culture and scientific culture are significantly different.

Science and Cultural Anthropology

One challenge for a scientific cultural anthropology is to forge comparable concepts. There are two parts to the problem. One is whether we can construct concepts that are not embedded in only one natural culture, or in any natural culture at all, the problem of cultural contamination. The other part is the construction of a lexicon to name those concepts that does not contain ambiguity. This book is an attempt to try the strategy of dimensions and

objects used in natural science to see if it provides any traction on the problems our discipline tackles.

My findings are that the discipline has been doing exactly that for over a
century and that it has been successful. But there is no written evidence (that
I have found) that we have been doing this consciously, although some
scholars seem to come very close to it (Ward Goodenough in particular).

A pivotal example of an ambiguity that makes a difference can be found
with the term *culture*. There is a major ambiguity in the use of this in anthropology. Culture1 is my label for a definition of culture which refers to
those behaviors and thoughts which are learned by humans from other humans. This definition was expressed by Tylor in 1871 and has been used by
many ever since. Culture2 refers to the set of beliefs and symbols which are
learned by humans from other humans. This meaning of culture is only a part
of culture1. Although culture2 has roots deep in the past it has became the
dominant meaning for a large number of anthropologists only since World
War II. It is strongly connected with the worldview of Talcott Parsons, and
two people trained at Harvard during Parsons's dominance, David Schneider
and Clifford Geertz, became the major proponents of this position in American anthropology.

This ambiguity is important in our consideration of comparability. If anthropology studies culture, and if culture means culture2, then it is difficult
to construct scientific approaches. If, on the other hand, by culture we mean
culture1, then scientific approaches are much easier to construct. It is necessary, or so I claim, to keep the differences between culture1 and culture2 clear
and at the forefront of consciousness. The ambiguity has been marked lexi-
cally and has (I hope) been eliminated from the text.

The distinction between folk concepts and scientific concepts is central to
my tale. Folk concepts are those ideas and meanings that the members of a
natural culture discuss in the natural language(s) of their natural culture
(culture2). Scientific concepts are constructed in a scientific culture, not a
natural one, and consciously have many features that are rare to absent in
natural cultures. These features include dimensions, objects, unique naming,
standards for calibration, and systematic training, all the products of a
process of construction that is recorded in the literature and open to challenge. Scientific concepts of culture can be about any aspect of culture1.
They can apply to matters that the members of that natural culture talk
about all the time. They can also apply to aspects of what they do that are far
from consciousness (for them).

A number of anthropologists apparently believe that there are only folk
concepts and that what the rest of us call science (including anthropology)

is only the folk concepts of a particular natural culture, the West. Adherents of culture2 are prominent in this regard. From their viewpoint it is not possible to construct scientific concepts in the realm of culture.

Scientific Concepts in Cultural Anthropology

Having argued for the reality of culture1, for the reality of scientific concepts, and for a strategy of using objects and dimensions for scientific observation, my discussion then turned to some examples from cultural anthropology.

The first example was the phonological structure of human languages. There is no known natural culture which has folk concepts for these phenomena, and yet they are learned from speakers of a natural language. They therefore are part of culture1 but are not part of culture2.

The observational language (encoded in the International Phonetic Alphabet) is a scientific composite of all the sounds that the human vocal tract can make. Cultural contamination of the observation language is avoided because natural constants are involved, as the sounds are defined in terms of common features of the anatomy of the vocal tract. There are no tangible standards, such as a thermometer. Instead a material model of sound production, the human vocal tract, is used. Intensive training in an apprentice environment is necessary, and once mastered, constant practice is necessary to keep the observational skills sharp.

There have been conventions (held by the International Phonetic Association—the last in Kiel in 1989) that discuss matters of theory, nomenclature, and representation and that result in new formulations of the subject matter. The Kiel convention was called because of tension between two theories, of phonic segments and of distinctive features. Clearly the underlying theory is not yet crystal clear and accepted by everybody, and the IPA is a work in progress.

But there is general agreement that the etic roster is based on the anatomy of the vocal tract (natural constants), that we need unambiguous names for the parts of that etic roster, and that natural languages select only some of the possibilities from this etic roster. We have a mature scientific observation language that has achieved dimensions based on natural constants, are the same kind of thing, and have an unambiguous naming system. It is a work in progress, and it has progressed quite far. To this outsider it seems like there is not much left to be accomplished—there are some details left to straighten out.

The second example presented is ethnotaxonomy. (There surely is much more to ethnobiology than taxonomy—anatomy, behavior, and ecology come to mind, just as there is more to ethnoscience than ethnobiology.) In this case we have two well-developed observation languages—linguistics (phonology, morphology, semantics) and botanical and zoological taxonomy. Each has natural constants to base kinds of things on, and each has procedures for reducing and controlling ambiguity. Each has its own set of procedures and training systems.

They are applied to the way that members of a natural culture assign lexicon to kinds of plants and animals. The major logistical problem seems to be the conjunction of scientific experts in the locale of the natural culture. Once that is accomplished there seem to be few barriers to getting the work done. Some interesting problems deserve investigation, such as ambiguity in the natural language and the nature and role of natural culture "expertise" and "expert." There are few people equipped by training and temperament to do this work, but the results seem solid.

The third example is agricultural productivity. By no means do all natural cultures contain agriculture. For those that do, we can ask about the productivity of land and labor, and we can get answers. Several observational languages are needed, including time, length, mass, plant names, and tool kits. All of these are well developed, and with one exception there seems to be little cultural contamination or ambiguity. The one exception is labor—the definitions in use produce an uncomfortably high level of uncertainty. The central problem here seems to be not the natural culture behavior but the lack of interest on the part of investigators in establishing standards.

There is another visible problem in this field, finding a general concept of crop output. Humans grow many different crops for many different purposes. Some are desired as the main source of calories, some for protein, some for taste, some for decoration, some for fibers. Ecologists like to discuss outputs with energy, but the energy in a chili pepper is trivial. One can capture variation in outputs of the major energy crops (rice, wheat, maize, etc.) in a useful way, but there is as yet no way to combine the output values of chili peppers, cotton, and rice. The economic solution is to measure all outputs in prices, but this works well only where there are markets and money. We are left with a conceptual problem in comparability, measuring the value of all crops simultaneously, that has not been solved. It may be the case that it can never be solved, unlike the labor concept problem.

The fourth example is the social organization of canal irrigation. Unlike the other examples, this one has received systematic attention from only a few scholars, so there are no shoulders of an old and rich literature to stand upon. Instead it involves the results of a single research effort. I have consciously tried to construct scientific concepts that solve for cultural contamination and ambiguity. Whether I have succeeded is not for me to say, at least at this moment.

The final example is kinship. This is perhaps the oldest topic in modern anthropology and occupied much of the problem-solving abilities of most anthropologists for close to a century. Problems of cultural contamination and ambiguity plagued the early efforts, but it is clear that enormous progress has been made. Concepts of natural constants have been developed, including kin types, kin terms, and roles. It is thought by some that all natural cultures have or contain kinship.

In the 1970s and 1980s there were strongly phrased skeptical retreats by Needham and Schneider. Schneider argued that the anthropological concept of "kinship" was not a scientific (he used "analytic") term and was instead a culturally contaminated projection from the natural culture of Euro-America. He used materials from Yap in an attempt to prove his point. His views are contentious, some accepting and some rejecting them. I have argued that he made errors in projecting his views of American kinship on to anthropologists and that his presentation of Yap ethnography does not support his view that the Yapese do not have a concept of kinship. There are a few critical points in the controversy that could be resolved with more field data from Yap.

Argument has been fierce over whether *kinship* denotes a single kind of cultural thing. I accept the position that kinship can be so defined. I think that the genetrix–child birth link is a very strong candidate for the natural constant. Networks of birth links seem to be very widely and perhaps universally found in natural cultures. Their functional load of course varies (and that variation ought to be investigated). We have an observation language (kin types), and we have had the capacity to train apprentices in how to use it. Ambiguity is much higher than it needs to be but is surely a result of a refusal to recognize the need for reducing it rather than being inherent in the subject matter.

One can reasonably ask if these five examples are the only ones possible. If the answer is yes, then optimism about a science of culture would seem to be questionable. I hold, to the contrary, that there are many examples: color terms; tool manufacture; making, controlling, and using fire; division of labor by sex; the incest taboo; socialization of infants and children; economic exchange; property; status and role; inequality; conflict resolution. For each of these there are substantial literatures both ethnographic and comparative. For each of these we know a great deal about similarity and difference. For each of these we have a set of correlations with other dimensions. I suggest that dimensions and objects are widely found in studies of culture1 and that the problems with developing further a science of culture are to be found in us rather than in nature. (We have met the enemy, and he is us?)

Where Are We?

This work is about the problem of comparability in cultural anthropology. I have argued that the natural sciences had to face this problem, and have used dimensions and objects. In both cases cultural contamination and ambiguity have been overcome by social means. Explicit concepts, often anchored in natural constants, and deliberately unambiguous language have been achieved, and deliberately so. There is much yet to be understood concerning why these systems are so stable across space and time, but there is little doubt that they work. SI is the most prominent example, but there are dozens of other examples both in the sciences (e.g., organisms, molecules) and in commerce (e.g., COLREGS, INCOTERMS). In most cases there is some international organization which has procedures for deciding on concepts and names. Why the rest of the world accepts these is the question. Semantic drift has been brought under conscious control, and it is a substantial victory over a powerful force of nature.

Having identified some principles in use in natural science, the next task was to see if those principles applied in the case of cultural anthropology. Always assuming culture1, I find that they have been useful in at least some instances. I do not claim that the entirety of the local reality project requires, or would even benefit, from these strategies. But for the comparative projects of cultural anthropology I think the case has been made. The dimensional approach seems to work.

Objects, however, are another story. These are clearly more problematic, at least in the details of our understanding. It may be the case that our speculations about cultures, societies, communities, and so forth are in fact quite valid. But there has as yet been no effort to test these propositions, and they remain uncomfortably vague and dissociated from rigorous scholarship.

I have argued that achieving cross-cultural comparability for culture1 is not only possible, it is in fact being done. The conclusion that this leads to, at least for me, is that *if* we use culture1, and *if* we work at solving problems of cultural contamination and ambiguity, we can achieve comparability of observations. It seems to me that methodological optimism is warranted. We have come a long way over the centuries. We have succeeded in creating a culture of science, and more to the point, a science of culture. There is reason to be optimistic about science in general, and social science in particular.

We *can* compare apples and oranges.

References Cited

Aberle, D. F., A. K. Cohen, A. K. Davis, M. J. Levy Jr., and F. X. Sutton. 1950. The functional prerequisites of society. *Ethics* 60:100–111.

Adams, John Quincy. 1821. *Report of the Secretary of State Upon Weights and Measures.* House Document 109 of the 16th Congress. Washington, DC: Gales and Seaton. Reprinted 1980, New York: Arno Press.

Adams, Robert McC. 1966. *The evolution of urban society: Early Mesopotamia and pre-hispanic Mexico.* Chicago: Aldine Press.

Adams, William Y., and Ernest W. Adams. 1991. *Archaeological typology and practical reality: A dialectical approach to artifact classification and sorting.* Cambridge: Cambridge University Press.

Alder, Ken. 2002. *The measure of all things: The seven-year odyssey and hidden error that transformed the world.* New York: The Free Press.

Ambrose, Stanley H. 2001. Paleolithic technology and human evolution. *Science* 291:1748–1753.

Atran, Scott. 1990. *Cognitive foundations of natural history: Towards an anthropology of science.* Cambridge: Cambridge University Press.

Banton, Michael. 1965. *Roles: An introduction to the study of social relations.* New York: Basic Books.

Barkin, David, and T. King. 1970. *Regional economic development: The river basin approach.* Cambridge: Cambridge University Press.

Bayliss-Smith, T. P. 1982. *The ecology of agricultural systems.* Cambridge: Cambridge University Press.

Beardsley, Richard K. 1963. Ecological and social parallels between rice-growing communities in Japan and Spain. In *Symposium on Community Studies in Anthropology*

(V. Garfield and E Friedl, eds.), 51–63. Proceedings, Annual Spring Meeting, American Ethnological Society, Seattle, American Ethnological Society.

Beardsley, Richard K., John W. Hall, and Robert E. Ward. 1959. *Village Japan*. Chicago: University of Chicago Press.

Behrens, Clifford. 1989. Relationships between Shipibo and western soil classification: Changes in land use patterns with cash cropping. *American Anthropologist* 91:83–100.

Bender, Donald. 1967. A refinement of the concept of household: Families, coresidence, and domestic functions. *American Anthropologist* 69:493–504.

Berlin, Brent. 1992. *Ethnobiological classification: Principles of categorization of plants and animals in traditional societies*. Princeton, NJ: Princeton University Press.

Berlin, Brent, Dennis E. Breedlove, and Peter H. Raven. 1974. *Principles of Tzeltal plant classification: An introduction to the botanical ethnography of Mayan-speaking people of highland Chiapas*. New York: Academic Press.

Bernard, H. Russell. 2002. *Research methods in anthropology*. Walnut Creek, CA: AltaMira Press.

Berndt, Ronald M. 1959. The concept of "the tribe" in the western desert of Australia. *Oceania* 30:81–107.

———. 1976. Territoriality and the problem of demarcating sociocultural space. In *Tribes and Boundaries in Australia* (Nick Peterson, ed.), 133–161. Canberra: Australian Institute of Aboriginal Studies, Behavior Science Research.

Bohannan, Paul. 1963. *Social anthropology*. New York: Holt Rinehart and Winston.

Bohannan, Paul, and Laura Bohannan. 1968. *Tiv economy*. Evanston, IL: Northwestern University Press.

Bolton, Ralph. 1977. The Qolla marriage process. In *Andean Kinship and Marriage* (R. Bolton and E. Mayer, eds.) 217–239. Special Publication #7. Washington, DC: American Anthropological Association.

Boserup, Ester. 1965. *The conditions of agricultural growth*. Chicago: Aldine Press.

Bowen, Elenore Smith. 1954. *Return to laughter*. New York: Harper.

Bronson, Bennett. 1972. Farm labor and the evolution of food production. In *Population Growth* (B. Spooner, ed.), 190–218. Cambridge, MA: MIT Press.

Brown, Donald E. 1991. *Human universals*. Philadelphia, PA: Temple University Press.

Carneiro, Robert. 1961. Slash-and-burn cultivation among the Kuikuru and its implications for cultural development in the Amazon. In *The Evolution of Horticultural Systems in Native North America* (J. Wilbert, ed.), 47–67. Sociedad de Ciencias Naturales La Salle, Editorial Sucre, Caracas.

Carrier, James G. 1992. Occidentalism: the world turned upside down. *American Ethnologist* 19:195–212.

———. 1995. Maussian occidentalism: Gift and commodity systems. In *Occidentalism: Images of the West* (James G. Carrier, ed.), 85–108. Oxford: Clarendon Press.

Chisholm, Lawrence J. 2002. Measurement systems. *The New Encyclopaedia Britannica* 23:693–697.

COLREGS. 1972. Convention on the International Regulations for Preventing Collisions at Sea, 1972. London: International Maritime Organization.

Conklin, Harold. 1957. *Hanunóo agriculture: A report on the integral system of shifting cultivation in the Philippines*. Rome: FAO (1975 reprint, Northford, CT: Elliot's Books).

Count, Earl W. 1973. *Being and becoming human: Essays on the biogram*. New York: Van Nostrand Reinhold.

Coward, E. Walter. 1976. Indigenous organization, bureaucracy and development: The case of irrigation. *Journal of Development Studies* 13:92–105.

———. 1979. Principles of social organization in an indigenous irrigation system. *Human Organization* 38:28–36.

———. 1980. Management themes in community irrigation systems. In *Irrigation and Agricultural Development in Asia* (E. W. Coward, ed.), 203–218. Ithaca, NY: Cornell University Press.

Cronk, L. 1999. *That complex whole: Culture and the evolution of human behavior*. Boulder, CO: Westview Press.

Crump, Thomas. 1990. *The anthropology of numbers*. Cambridge: Cambridge University Press.

Custred, Glynn. 1977. Peasant kinship, subsistence and economies in a high altitude Andean environment. In *Andean Kinship and Marriage* (R. Bolton and E. Mayer, eds.), 117–136. Washington, DC: American Anthropological Association.

Damon, Frederick H. 1986. Review of *A Critique of Kinship* by D. M. Schneider. *American Anthropologist* 88:234–235.

D'Andrade, Roy. 1995. Moral models in anthropology. *Current Anthropology* 36(3):399–408.

———. 1999. Culture is not everything. In *Anthropological Theory in North America* (E. L. Cerroni-Long, ed.), 85–103. Westport, CT: Bergin & Garvey.

Darton, Mike, and John Clark. 1994. *The Macmillan dictionary of measurement*. New York: Macmillan Publishing Company.

Desowitz, Robert S. 1991. *The malaria capers: Tales of parasites and people*. New York: W. W. Norton Co.

Dilke, O. A. W. 1987. *Reading the past: Mathematics and measurement*. London: The British Museum Press.

Doolittle, William. 1990. *Canal irrigation in prehispanic Mexico*. Austin: University of Texas Press.

Durrenberger, E. Paul. 1978. *Agricultural production and household budgets in a Shan peasant village in northwestern Thailand: A quantitative description*. Southeast Asia Studies 49. Athens, OH: Ohio University Center for International Studies, Southeast Asia Program.

Earle, Timothy. 1978. *Economic and social organization of a complex chiefdom: The Halaelea district, Kauai, Hawaii*. Anthropological Paper 63. Ann Arbor: Museum of Anthropology, University of Michigan.

Eggan, Fred. 1950. *The social organization of the western pueblos*. Chicago: University of Chicago Press.

Ellen, Roy. 1982. *Environment, subsistence and system: The ecology of small-scale social formations.* Cambridge: Cambridge University Press.

Ember, Carol. 1983. The relative decline in women's contribution to agriculture with intensification. *American Anthropologist* 85:285–304.

Ember, Carol, and David Levinson. 1991. The substantive contributions of worldwide cross-cultural studies using secondary data. In *Cross-Cultural and Comparative Research: Theory and Method. Behavior Science Research* 25:79–140.

Fairen Guillen, Victor. 1975. *El tribunal de las Aguas de Valencia, y su proceso.* Valencia, Spain: Caja de Ahorros y Monte de Piedad de Valencia.

Feinberg, Richard, and Martin Ottenheimer (eds.). 2001. *The cultural analysis of kinship: The legacy of David M. Schneider.* Urbana: University of Illinois Press.

Fernea, Robert. 1970. *Shaykh and Effendi.* Cambridge, MA: Harvard University Press.

Flowers, Jeff. 2004. The route to atomic and quantum standards. *Science* 306:1324–1330.

Freeman, Derek. 1955. *Iban agriculture.* Colonial Research Studies 18. London: Her Majesty's Stationery Office (reprinted 1980, New York: AMS Press).

Geertz, Clifford. 1973. *The interpretation of cultures.* New York: Basic Books.

———. 1983. *Local knowledge.* New York: Basic Books.

Gelles, Paul. 1984. Agua, faenas, y organización communal en los Andes: El caso de San Pedro de Casta. Master's thesis, Universidad Catolica Lima.

Gelman, Rochel, and C. R. Gallistel. 2004. Language and the origin of numerical concepts. *Science* 306:441–443.

Goodenough, Ward H. 1965. Rethinking 'status' and 'role': Towards a general model of the cultural organization of social relationships. In *The Relevance of Models for Social Anthropology,* 1–24. ASA Monographs 1. London: Tavistock Publications.

———. 1970. *Description and comparison.* Chicago: Aldine Press.

———. 1996. Culture. In *Encyclopedia of Cultural Anthropology* (D. Levinson and M. Ember, eds.), vol. 1, 291–299. New York: Henry Holt and Co.

Goody, Jack. 1976. *Production and reproduction: A comparative study of the domestic domain.* Cambridge: Cambridge University Press.

Gordon, Peter. 2004. Numerical cognition without words: Evidence from Amazonia. *Science* 306:496–499.

Gough, Kathleen. 1952. Changing kinship usages in the setting of political and economic change among the Nayar of Malabar. *Journal of the Royal Anthropological Institute* 82:71–88.

———. 1959. The Nayar and the definition of marriage. *Journal of the Royal Anthropological Institute* 89:23–34.

Gould, Stephen J. 2000. Deconstructing the "science wars" by reconstructing an old mold. *Science* 287:253–261.

Gould, Sydney H. 2000. *A new system for the formal analysis of kinship.* Lanham, MD: University Press of America.

Grimes, Barbara (ed.). 1996. *Ethnologue: Languages of the world.* Dallas, TX: Summer Institute of Linguistics.

Gross, Daniel, and Stuart Plattner. 2002. Anthropology as social work: Collaborative models of anthropological research. *Anthropology News* 43(8):4.

Guillet, David. 1992. *Covering ground: Communal water management and the state in the Peruvian highlands*. Ann Arbor: University of Michigan Press.

Hanks, Lucien. 1972. *Rice and man*. Chicago: Aldine Atherton Inc.

Hanson, F. Allen. 1975. *Meaning in culture*. London: Routledge and Kegan Paul.

Harris, Marvin. 1979. *Cultural materialism: The struggle for a science of culture*. New York: Random House.

———. 1999. *Theories of culture in postmodern times*. Walnut Creek, CA: AltaMira Press.

Hawkes, Kristin, and J. F. O'Connell. 1981. Affluent hunters? Some comments in the light of the Alyawara case. *American Anthropologist* 83:622–626.

Headland, Thomas N., K. L. Pike, and M. R. Harris (eds.). 1990. *Emics and etics: The insider/outsider debate*. Newbury Park, CA: Sage.

Hoenigswald, Henry M., and Linda F. Wiener. 1987. *Biological metaphor and cladistic classification: An interdisciplinary interpretation*. Philadelphia: University of Pennsylvania Press.

Hull, David. 1992. Biological species: An inductivist's nightmare. In *How Classification Works* (M. Douglas and D. Hull, eds.), 42–68. Edinburgh: Edinburgh University Press.

Hunn, Eugene. 1977. *Tzeltal folk zoology: The classification of discontinuities in nature*. New York: Academic Press.

———. 1996. Ethnozoology. In *Encyclopedia of Cultural Anthropology* (D. Levinson and M. Ember, eds.), vol. 2, 451–456. New York: Henry Holt and Co.

Hunt, Eva V. 1969. Kinship in San Juan: Genealogical and social models. *Ethnology* 8:37–53.

Hunt, Robert C. 1971. Components of relationships in the family: A Mexican village. In *Kinship and Culture* (Francis L. K. Hsu, ed.), 106–143. Chicago: Aldine Press.

———. 1986. Canal irrigation in Egypt: Common property management. In Proceedings of the Conference on Common Property Resource Management, 199–214. Washington, DC: National Academy Press.

———. 1988a. CA comment on Jane I. Guyer, The multiplication of labor. *Current Anthropology* 29:247–272.

———. 1988b. Size and the structure of authority in canal irrigation systems. *Journal of Anthropological Research* 44:335–355.

———. 1995. Agrarian data sets: The comparativist's view. In *The Comparative Analysis of Human Societies: Toward Common Standards for Data Collection and Reporting* (E. Moran, ed.), 173–189. Boulder, CO: Lynne Rienner.

———. 2000. Labor productivity and agricultural development: Boserup revisited. *Human Ecology* 28(2):251–277.

———. 2001. Irrigation: Management and "reform." *International Journal of Water* 1:397–400.

———. 2006. Locally controlled irrigation systems: Principles and practices. In *A World of Water: Rain, Rivers and Seas in Southeast Asian Histories* (Peter Boomgaard, ed.), 187–208. Leiden: KITLV Press.

Hunt, Robert C., David Guillet, David Abbott, James Bayman, Paul Fish, Suzanne Fish, Keith Kintigh, and James Neely. 2005. Plausible ethnographic analogies for the organization of Hohokam irrigation. *American Antiquity* 70(3):433–456.

Hunt, Robert C., and Eva V. Hunt. 1976. Canal irrigation and local social organization. *Current Anthropology* 17:389–411.

Hymes, Dell. 1968. Linguistic problems in defining the concept of "tribe." In *Essays in the Problem of Tribe* (J. Helm, ed.), 23–48. Proceedings of the Annual Spring Meeting, American Ethnological Society.

INCOTERMS. International Chamber of Commerce, World Business Organization, pub. 460. Paris: International Chamber of Commerce.

Ingold, Tim, David Riches, and James Woodburn (eds.). 1988. *Hunters and Gatherers*, vols. 1, 2. New York: Berg.

International Commission on Zoological Nomenclature. 2000. *International code of zoological nomenclature*. 4th ed. London: International Commission on Zoological Nomenclature.

International Phonetic Association. 1999. *Handbook of the international phonetic association*. Cambridge: Cambridge University Press.

Jacobson, David. 1991. *Reading ethnography*. Stony Brook: State University of New York Press.

Janlekha, Kamol Odd. 1955. *A study of the economy of a rice growing village in central Thailand*. Bangkok: Ministry of Agriculture, Division of Agricultural Economics.

Jha, Nitish. 2001. The bifurcate Subak: The social organization of a Balinese irrigation community. Ph.D. dissertation, Brandeis University.

———. 2002. Barriers to the diffusion of knowledge: A Balinese case. In *Economic Development* (J. Cohen and N. Dannhaeuser, eds.), 87–106. Walnut Creek, CA: AltaMira Press.

———. 2004. Gender and decision making in Balinese agriculture. *American Ethnologist* 31:552–572.

Johnson, Allen W., and Timothy Earle. 1987. *The evolution of human societies: From foraging group to agrarian state*. Stanford: Stanford University Press.

Johnson, Nels. 2001. Managing water for people and nature. *Science* 292:1071–1072.

Kaplan, David. 2000. The darker side of the "Original Affluent Society." *Journal of Anthropological Research* 56:301–324.

Kaplan, David, and Robert A. Manners. 1972. *Culture theory*. Englewood Cliffs, NJ: Prentice–Hall.

Kappel, W. 1974. Irrigation development and population pressure. In *Irrigation's impact on society* (T. Downing and M. Gibson, eds.), 159–168. Tucson: University of Arizona Press.

Keesing, Roger. 1974. Theories of culture. *Annual Review of Anthropology* 3:73–98.

———. 1975. *Kin groups and social structure*. New York: Holt Rinehart and Winston.

———. 1989. Exotic reading of cultural texts. *Current Anthropology* 30(4):459–479.

Kelly, William. 1983. Concepts in the anthropological study of irrigation. *American Anthropologist* 85:880–886.

Kendall, Timothy. 1986. *The cubit rule*. Newton Lower Falls, MA: Ostracon Antiquarian Delights.

Kestenbaum, David. 1998. Recipe for a kilogram. *Science* 280:823–824.

Kilborne, Benjamin, and L. L. Langness (eds.). 1987. *Culture and human nature: Theoretical papers of Melford E. Spiro.* Chicago: University of Chicago Press.

Klein, H. Arthur. 1974. *The world of measurements.* New York: Simon and Schuster.

Kroeber, Alfred E. 1909. Classificatory systems of relationship. *Journal of the Royal Anthropological Institute* 39:77–84.

Kroeber, Alfred E., and Talcott Parsons. 1958. The concept of culture and of social systems. *American Sociological Review* 23:582–583.

Kundstadter, Peter, E. C. Chapman, and Sanga Sabhasri (eds.). 1978. *Farmers in the forest: Economic development and marginal agriculture in northern Thailand.* Honolulu: University Press of Hawaii.

Kuper, Adam. 1999. *Culture: The anthropologist's account.* Cambridge, MA: Harvard University Press.

Kuznar, Lawrence A. 1997. *Reclaiming a scientific anthropology.* Walnut Creek, CA: AltaMira Press.

Labby, D. 1976. *The demystification of Yap: Dialectics of culture on a Micronesian island.* Chicago: University of Chicago Press.

Ladefoged, Peter. 1990. The revised International Phonetic Alphabet. *Language* 66:550–552.

Ladefoged, Peter, and Morris Halle. 1988. Some major features of the International Phonetic Alphabet. *Language* 64:577–582.

Lagace, Robert O. 1967. Principles and procedures of ethnographic unit identification, with particular reference to the HRAF files system. *Behavior Science Notes* 2:89–103.

Lakoff, George. 1987. *Women, fire and dangerous things: What categories reveal about the mind.* Chicago: University of Chicago Press.

Lambert, Bernd. 1977. Bilaterality in the Andes. In *Andean Kinship and Marriage* (R. Bolton and E. Mayer, eds.), 1–27. Washington, DC: American Anthropological Association.

Lansing, S. 1991. *Priests and programmers.* Princeton, NJ: Princeton University Press.

Lass, Roger. 1984. *Phonology: An introduction to basic concepts.* Cambridge: Cambridge University Press.

Leach, Edmund R. 1961a. *Pul Eliya.* Cambridge: Cambridge University Press.

———. 1961b. *Rethinking anthropology.* London School of Economics Monographs on Social Anthropology 22. London: Athlone Press.

———. 1965. The comparative method in anthropology. In *International Encyclopaedia of the Social Sciences* (E. Shills, ed.), vol. 1, 339–345.

Leacock, Eleanor, and Richard Lee (eds.). 1982. *Politics and history in band societies.* Cambridge: Cambridge University Press.

Lee, Richard. 1988. *The Dobe Kung.* Fort Worth, TX: Holt Rinehart and Winston.

Lee, Richard, and Irven DeVore (eds.). 1968. *Man the hunter.* Chicago: Aldine Press.

Lehman, Fritz K. 1985. Cognition and computation: On being sufficiently abstract. In *Directions in Cognitive Anthropology* (Janet W. D. Dougherty, ed.), 19–48. Urbana: University of Illinois Press.

Lett, James. 1987. *The human enterprise: A critical introduction to anthropological theory.* Boulder, CO: Westview Press.

———. 1990. Emics and etics: Notes on the epistemology of anthropology. In *Emics and Etics: The Insider/Outsider Debate* (T. Headland, K. L. Pike, and M. R. Harris, eds.), 127–142. Newbury Park, CA: Sage.

———. 1997. *Science, reason, and anthropology.* Lanham, MD: Rowman & Littlefield.

Levine, Donald. 1985. *The flight from ambiguity: Essays in social and cultural theory.* Chicago: University of Chicago Press.

Levinson, David, and Martin J. Malone. 1980. *Toward explaining human culture: A critical review of the findings of worldwide cross-cultural research.* New Haven, CT: HRAF Press.

Lingenfelter, S. G. 1975. *Yap: Political leadership and culture change in an island society.* Honolulu: University Press of Hawaii.

Linklater, Andro. 2002. *Measuring America.* New York: Walker and Co.

Linton, Ralph. 1936. *The study of man.* New York: Appleton.

Loker, William. 1988. Weights and measures: Methodological issues in the estimation of agricultural productivity. *Culture and Agriculture* 35:13–17.

Maass, Arthur, and Raymond L. Anderson. 1978. *. . . and the desert shall rejoice.* Cambridge, MA: MIT Press.

Maclachlan, Morgan. 1983. *Why they did not starve: Biocultural adaptation in a South Indian village.* Philadelphia, PA: Institute for the Study of Human Issues.

Malinowski, Bronislaw. 1967. *A diary in the strict sense of the term.* London: Routledge and Kegan Paul.

McGrew, W. C. 1998. Culture in nonhuman primates? *Annual Review of Anthropology* 27:301–328.

Middleton, W. W. Knowles. 1964. *The history of the barometer.* Baltimore: Johns Hopkins University Press.

———. 1966. *A history of the thermometer and its use in meteorology.* Baltimore: Johns Hopkins University Press.

Millon, René. 1962. Variations in social response to the practice of irrigated agriculture. In *Civilization in Desert Lands* (R. Woodbury, ed.), 56–88. Anthropology Papers 62. Salt Lake City: University of Utah.

Moerman, Michael. 1965. Who are the Lue? *American Anthropologist* 67:1215–1230.

———. 1968a. *Agricultural change and peasant choice in a Thai village.* Berkeley: University of California Press.

———. 1968b. Being Lue: Uses and abuses of ethnic identification. In *Essays in the Problem of Tribe* (J. Helm, ed.), 153–169. Proceedings of the Annual Spring Meeting, American Ethnological Society.

Montague, Susan P. 2001. The Trobriand kinship classification and Schneider's cultural relativism. In *The Cultural Analysis of Kinship: The Legacy of David M. Schnei-*

der (Richard Feinberg and Martin Ottenheimer, eds.), 168–186. Urbana: University of Illinois Press.

Moran, Emilio. 1986. Comment on "Weights and measures and swidden." *Culture and Agriculture* 29:7–8.

Moran, Emilio (ed.). 1995. *The comparative analysis of human societies: Toward common standards for data collection and reporting.* Boulder, CO: Lynne Rienner.

Morgan, Lewis Henry. 1871. *Systems of consanguinity and affinity of the human family.* Washington, DC: Smithsonian Institution.

Murdock, George Peter. 1949. *Social structure.* New York: Macmillan.

Murdock, George P., and Douglas R. White. 1969. Standard cross-cultural sample. *Ethnology* 8:329–369.

Nadel, Siegfried. 1957. *The theory of social structure.* Glencoe, IL: The Free Press.

Naroll, Raoul. 1964. On ethnic unit classification. *Current Anthropology* 5:283–312.

———. 1968. Who the Lue are. In *Essays in the Problem of Tribe* (J. Helm, ed.), 72–82. Proceedings of the Annual Spring Meeting, American Ethnological Society.

———. 1970a. The culture-bearing unit in cross-cultural surveys. In *A Handbook of Method in Cultural Anthropology* (R. Naroll and R. Cohen, eds.), 721–765. Garden City, NY: Natural History Press.

———. 1970b. What have we learned from cross-cultural surveys? *American Anthropologist* 72:1227–1288.

Needham, Rodney. 1971a. Introduction. In *Rethinking Kinship and Marriage* (R. Needham, ed.), xii–cxvii. ASA vol. 11. London: Tavistock Publications.

———. 1971b. Remarks on the analysis of kinship and marriage. In *Rethinking Kinship and Marriage* (R. Needham, ed.), 1–34. ASA vol. 11. London: Tavistock Publications.

———. (ed.). 1971c. *Rethinking kinship and marriage.* ASA vol. 11. London: Tavistock Publications.

———. 1975. Polythetic classification: Convergence and consequences. *MAN* (N.S.) 10:349–369.

Netting, Robert McC. 1974. The system nobody knows: Village irrigation in the Swiss Alps. In *Irrigation's Impact on Society* (T. Downing and M. Gibson, eds.), 67–76. Tucson: University of Arizona Press.

O'Meara, Tim. 1997. Causation and the struggle for a science of culture. *Current Anthropology* 38(3):399–418.

———. 1999. Causal individualism and the unification of anthropology. In *Anthropological Theory in North America* (E. L. Cerroni-Long, ed.), 105–141. Westport, CT: Bergin & Garvey.

———. 2001. Causation and the postmodern critique of objectivity. *Anthropological Theory* 1(1):31–56.

Ostrom, Elinor. 1990. *Governing the commons: The evolution of institutions for collective action.* Cambridge: Cambridge University Press.

Ottenheimer, Martin. 2001. Relativism in kinship analysis. In *The Cultural Analysis of Kinship: The Legacy of David M. Schneider* (Richard Feinberg and Martin Ottenheimer, eds.), 118–139. Urbana: University of Illinois Press.

Palerm-Viquera, Jacinta. 2001. Organizational strategies in situations of water scarcity: Self–administered irrigation systems in Mexico. *International Journal of Water* 1:285–306.

Parkin, Robert. 1997. *Kinship: An introduction to basic concepts.* Oxford: Blackwell.

Pennisi, Elizabeth. 2001. Linnaeus's last stand? *Science* 291:2304–2307.

Pica, Pierre, C. Lemer, V. Izard, and S. Dehaene. 2004. Exact and approximate arithmetic in an Amazonian indigene group. *Science* 306:499–503.

Powell, Marvin. 1989. Masse und gewichte. *Reallexikon der Assyriologie* 7:457–480.

——. 1990. Masse und gewichte. *Reallexikon der Assyriologie* 7:481–517.

Przeworski, Adam, and Henry Teune. 1970. *The logic of comparative social inquiry.* New York: John Wiley and Sons.

Pullum, Geoffrey, and William A. Ladusaw. 1986. *Phonetic symbol guide.* Chicago: University of Chicago Press.

Rabinow, P., and W. Sullivan (eds.). 1987. *Interpretive social science: A second look.* Los Angeles: University of California Press.

Radcliffe-Brown, A. R. 1940. On social structure. *Journal of the Royal Anthropological Institute* 81:15–22.

Rappaport, Roy. 1968. *Pigs for the ancestors.* New Haven, CT: Yale University Press.

Redfield, Robert. 1934. *Chan Kom: A Maya village.* Chicago: University of Chicago Press.

Reyna, Stephen P. 1994. Literary anthropology and the case against science. *MAN* 29:555–582.

Ride, W. D. L. 1999. Introduction. In *International Code of Zoological Nomenclature,* 4th ed., xix–xxix. Adopted by the International Union of Biological Sciences.

Rivière, P. G. 1971. Marriage: A reassessment. In *Rethinking Kinship and Marriage* (Rodney Needham, ed.), 57–74. ASA vol. 11. London: Tavistock Publications.

Roca, Iggy, and Wyn Johnson. 1999. *A course in phonology.* Oxford: Blackwell.

Ronfeldt, Ronald. 1973. *Atencingo: The politics of agrarian struggle in a Mexican ejido.* Stanford, CA: Stanford University Press.

Rosaldo, R. 1989. *Culture and truth: The remaking of social analysis.* Boston: Beacon Press.

Russell, Kenneth W. 1988. *After Eden: The behavioral ecology of early food production in the Near East and North Africa.* British Archaeological Reports, International Series 391. Oxford: British Archaeological Reports.

Sahlins, Marshall. 1972. *Stone age economics.* Chicago: Aldine Press.

Saler, Benson. 1993. *Conceptualizing religion.* Leiden: Brill.

Sapir, Edward A. 1929. The status of linguistics as a science. *Language* 5:207–214.

Scheffler, Harold W. 2001. *Filiation and affiliation.* Boulder, CO: Westview Press.

Schneider, David. 1953. Yap kinship terminology and kin groups. *American Anthropologist* 55:215–236.

——. 1957. Political organization, supernatural sanctions and the punishment of incest on Yap. *American Anthropologist* 59:791–800.

——. 1968. *American kinship.* Englewood Cliffs, NJ: Prentice-Hall.

———. 1984. *A critique of the study of kinship*. Ann Arbor: University of Michigan Press.

———. 1992. Ethnocentrism and the notion of kinship: Response to Shimuzu. *MAN* 27:629–631.

Scholte, Bob. 1984. Reason and culture: The universal and the particular revisited. *American Anthropologist* 86:960–965.

Schwartz, Norman. 1985. A note on weights, measures, and swidden. *Culture and Agriculture* 29:9–12.

Schweizer, Thomas, and Douglas R. White (eds.). 1998. *Kinship, networks and exchange*. Cambridge: Cambridge University Press.

Sen, Amartya. 1992. *Inequality reexamined*. Cambridge, MA: Harvard University Press.

Service, Elman. 1975. *Origins of the state and civilization: The process of cultural evolution*. New York: W. W. Norton Co.

———. 1985. *A century of controversy: Ethnological issues from 1860 to 1960*. Orlando, FL: Academic Press.

Shimuzu, Akitoshi. 1991. On the notion of kinship. *MAN* 26:377–403.

Sidky, H. 2003. *A critique of postmodern anthropology: In defense of disciplinary origins and traditions*. Lewiston, NY: Edwin Mellen Press.

Sneath, P., and R. Sokal. 1973. *Numerical taxonomy*. San Francisco: W. H. Freeman.

Southwold, Martin. 1971. Meanings of kinship. In *Rethinking Kinship and Marriage* (Rodney Needham, ed.), 35–56. ASA vol. 11. London: Tavistock Publications.

Sperber, Dan. 1996. *Explaining culture: A naturalistic approach*. Oxford: Blackwell.

Spiro, Melford. 1966. Religion: Problems of definition and explanation. In *Anthropological Approaches to the Study of Religion* (M. Banton, ed.), 85–126. London, Tavistock Publications. (Reprinted 1987 in *Culture and Human Nature: Theoretical Papers of Melford E. Spiro*, B. Kilborne and L. L. Langness [eds.], 187–222. Chicago: University of Chicago Press.)

———. 1982. *Oedipus in the Trobriands*. Chicago: University of Chicago Press.

———. 1984. Some reflections on cultural determinism and relativism with special reference to emotion and reason. In *Culture Theory: Essays on Mind, Self, and Emotion* (R. A. Shweder and R. LeVine, eds.), 323–346. Cambridge: Cambridge University Press.

———. 1986. Cultural anthropology and the future of anthropology. *Cultural Anthropology* 1:259–286.

Spooner, Brian. 1974. Irrigation and society: The Iranian plateau. In *Irrigation's Impact on Society* (T. Downing and M. Gibson, eds.), 43–57. Tucson: University of Arizona Press.

Stevens, S. S. 1946. On the theory of scales of measurement. *Science* 103:677–680.

Steward, Julian. 1949. Cultural causality and law: A trial formulation of early civilization. *American Anthropologist* 51:1–27.

Stone, Linda. 1997. *Kinship and gender: An introduction*. Boulder, CO: Westview Press.

Tambiah, Stanley. 1990. *Magic, science, religion and the scope of rationality*. Cambridge: Cambridge University Press.

Trautman, Thomas R. 1987. *Lewis Henry Morgan and the invention of kinship*. Berkeley: University of California Press.

Tyler, S. 1987. *The unspeakable: Discourse, dialogue, and rhetoric in the postmodern world*. Madison: University of Wisconsin Press.

Tylor, E. B. 1871. *Primitive culture: Researches into the development of mythology, philosophy, religion, language, art and custom*. London: J. Murray.

———. 1889. On a method of investigating the development of institutions: Applied to laws of marriage and descent. *Journal of the Royal Anthropological Institute of Great Britain and Ireland* 18:245–272.

Uphoff, Norman. 1986. *Getting the process right: Improving water management with farmer organization and participation*. Boulder, CO: Westview Press.

Van der Mere, Canute. 1968. Changing water control in a Taiwanese rice field irrigation system. *Annals of the Association of American Geographers* 58:720–747.

Vayda, Andrew P. 1989. Explaining why Marings fought. *Journal of Anthropological Research* 45(2):159–177.

Vries, J. de. 1974. *The Dutch rural economy in the golden age, 1500–1700*. New Haven, CT: Yale University Press.

Wade, Robert. 1988. *Village republics: Economic conditions for collective action in South India*. Cambridge: Cambridge University Press.

Wang, Chien-ru. 1997. *Canal irrigation systems governed by common property management rules*. Unpublished Ph.D. dissertation, Anthropology Department, Brandeis University.

Wax, Rosalie. 1971. *Doing fieldwork*. Chicago: University of Chicago Press.

Weiner, James F. 1988. Review of *A Critique of Kinship* by D. M. Schneider. *Oceania* 58:236–237.

Whiten, A., J. Goodall, W. C. McGrew, T. Nishida, V. Reynolds, Y. Sugiyama, C. E. G. Tutin, R. W. Wrangham, and C. Boesch. 1999. Cultures in chimpanzees. *Nature* 399:682–685.

Winch, Peter. 1958. *The idea of a social science and its relation to philosophy*. London: Routledge and Kegan Paul.

Winter, Irene J. 2000. Opening the eyes and opening the mouth: The utility of comparing images in worship in India and the Ancient Near East. In *Ethnography and Personhood* (M. Meister, ed.), 129–162. Jaipur: Rawat Publications.

Witkowski, Stanley. 1996. Language. In *Encyclopedia of Cultural Anthropology* (D. Levinson and M. Ember, eds.), vol. 2, 687–693. New York: Henry Holt and Co.

Wittfogel, Karl. 1957. *Oriental despotism*. New Haven, CT: Yale University Press.

Zupko, Ronald Edward. 1981. Italian weights and measures from the Middle Ages to the nineteenth century. Memoir of the American Philosophical Society, vol. 145. Philadelphia, PA: American Philosophical Society.

———. 1990. *Revolution in measurement: Western European measures since the age of science*. Memoir of the American Philosophical Society, vol. 186. Philadelphia, PA: American Philosophical Society.

~

Index

About the Author

Robert C. Hunt, an economic anthropologist, is Professor Emeritus of Anthropology at Brandeis University, where he taught from 1969 to 2002. Educated at Hamilton College (B.A.), The University of Chicago (M.A.), and Northwestern University (Ph.D.), he has conducted field work in Mexico and has done comparative research. He currently holds a Mellon Foundation Emeritus Fellowship supporting his work on the economy of Hohokam.

www.ingramcontent.com/pod-product-compliance
Lightning Source LLC
Chambersburg PA
CBHW062029270326
41929CB00014B/2370